PERSPECTIVES ON SOUTHERN AFRICA

The Revolt of the Hereros

The Revolt
of the Hereros

Jon M. Bridgman

UNIVERSITY OF CALIFORNIA PRESS
BERKELEY • LOS ANGELES • LONDON

University of California Press
Berkeley and Los Angeles, California

University of California Press, Ltd.
London, England

© 1981 by
The Regents of the University of California

Library of Congress Cataloging in Publication Data

Bridgman, Jon.
  The revolt of the Hereros.
  (Perspectives on Southern Africa ; 30)
  Bibliography: p.
  Includes index.
  1. Nambia—History—Herero Revolt. 1904-1907.
  2. Hereros—History. I. Title. II. Series.
DT714.B74 968.8′02 80-13965
ISBN 0-520-04113-5

Contents

Maps

Credits for Photographs

Numbers 1, 9, 13, 14 and 15 are from H. Bley, *South-West Africa under German Rule* (Northwestern University Press, Evanston, Ill., 1971). Numbers 2, 3, 4, 5, 6, 7, 11, and 12 are from Grosse Generalstab, *Die Kämpfe der deutschen Truppen in Südwestafrika*, 2 vols. (Berlin, 1906). Number 8 is from Theodor Leutwein's *Elf Jahre Gouverneur in Deutsch Südwest Afrika* (Berlin, 1906). Numbers 16, 18, and 19 are from Union of South Africa, *Report on the Natives in South West Africa and Their Treatment by Germany* (London, 1918; a Command Paper). Number 10 is from *Illustrated London News*, February 6, 1904. Number 17 is from *Illustrierte Zeitung*, August 22, 1907.

Introduction

FROM 1904 to 1907 the tribes in South West Africa, especially the Hereros, fought a heroic but futile war against their German masters. For all practical purposes this war has, in a little more than two generations, disappeared from history. To be sure, it is recorded in histories of Imperial Germany, but generally only as a footnote on imperial politics. Some mention of it is also made in histories of Western colonialism and imperialism, but even reasonably detailed histories of South West Africa give no more than a page or two to the war.[1] From the standpoint of the Germans and other Europeans the war was not important. It was an incident, and no more, in an imperial adventure which has now ended.

But if for a moment we look at these events through the eyes of the tribes that took part in them, and in particular the Hereros, then the war is not a mere incident but rather the greatest historical event which the tribes ever experienced. It was their Marathon, their Cannae, their Sedan, their Hiroshima. Even using the normal criterion by which wars are rated, that is, total casualties, the Herero Revolt is no minor affair. Though casualty figures are notoriously inaccurate, the total dead was probably greater than in the Boer War, the Crimean War, the Spanish American War, the Seven Weeks War, and a dozen or more other conflicts that were fought

1. In the best recent book on South West Africa—John H. Wellington, *South West Africa and Its Human Issues* (Oxford, 1967)—the whole history of the fighting is covered in eight pages.

1

between 1815 and 1914.[2] So, if for no other reason than its size, one might argue that the Herero Revolt deserves greater recognition than it has received. But the whole issue of size is relatively unimportant. More to the point is that we take much away from a people when we deny them their history, and it is not a mystical exaggeration to say that we thereby remove part of their essential humanity. Few Hereros today have more than a hazy idea about their national past, and even fewer Africans know anything about the Herero Revolt.

Against almost insuperable odds, the Hereros, and later the Hottentots, repeatedly defeated and humiliated German forces which, in terms of training, equipment and numbers, were a quantum leap ahead of the tribes. The reasons for the tribal victories are not difficult to discern. In the first place, they were armed, and consciously armed, with a sense of moral superiority. They were fighting for their land, for their gods, for their traditions, for their women. Aside from their conviction of fighting for a just cause, the tribal leadership showed a high degree of military sophistication which, when combined with their knowledge of the terrain, produced a measure of flexibility and mobility that the Germans could never match. Ultimately, of course, the superior resources and firepower of the Germans wore the tribes down and led to their destruction, but for three long years the Germans had to suffer almost continuous humiliation at the hands of what they regarded as inferior, half-naked black men.

In the Herero War the technology of the West encountered the stark elemental forces of nature, and Western technology initially proved to be deficient, although no one in Europe seemed to comprehend the implications. After all, the war took place thousands of miles away from Germany and attracted the interest of the German public only for brief moments when

2. In Lewis Richardson's classic study, *The Statistics of Deadly Quarrels* (Pittsburgh, 1960), only three wars from 1815 to 1914 are clearly of a different order of magnitude, to wit: the Taiping Rebellion, the American Civil War, and the Great War of La Plata, all of which had more than 300,000 killed in action. The Herero War is in the same general order of magnitude as twenty some wars fought during this "century of peace."

some spectacular reversal had to be explained. Yet there were profound lessons for the Germans and for other Europeans as well from this obscure war. The failures of the military in South West Africa strongly suggested that the training and education of the professional officer class, the pride of the Empire, was in some basic ways wanting. When the enemy failed to respond as the officers had been taught he would, a sense of confusion and bafflement seemed to come over most of the officers, coupled with a dull instinct to try the old formulas once again even in the face of repeated failure. And when the military maxims that the officers had been weaned upon were obviously and manifestly prescriptions for disaster, the only alternative that anyone could think of was to kill, to kill and destroy without pity and without any concern for the costs in terms of treasure or human life. The response of the European officer class in the opening weeks of the First World War was nothing more than the response of those few dozen German officers in South West Africa writ large.

To a sensitive observer the war might also have raised serious questions about the new technology and its impact on warfare. The cost of technological advances proved to be disconcertingly high. The firepower of the German army in 1904 was probably ten times what it had been in 1870, and a hundred times greater than it had been at the time of the Napoleonic wars; yet while all this new ability to kill was in theory an advantage, in practice it tended to burden the army with a vast liability, for it crippled its power of movement and maneuver. Modern weapons that could fire tons of ammunition in a day raised the problem of appeasing the voracious appetite for shells. But in a greater sense, technology tended to create "technological soldiers" who were more and more removed from nature and humanity. All problems were held to have a technological solution. If Africans refused to accept the blessings of European civilization peaceably then they must be forced to do so by arms; if military force did not convince them, then they must be extirpated, for they had shown themselves unworthy, or perhaps better, unwilling to live in the twentieth century. Such brutal ethnocentricity might well have warned those who had eyes to see that something was amiss in the heart of Europe.

Although the war is worth studying, it does pose special problems of historical analysis. We have a mass of German written records, but from the Herero side no more than a handful of letters, written for the most part in bastardized Dutch.[3] Beyond the official records there are a few journalists accounts, a few memoirs; in all, no more than bits and pieces. Still, the problem of reconstructing Herero history is far from hopeless, largely because the Germans were inveterate record-keepers, and they published long and detailed accounts of the fighting. To be sure, these accounts were written to explain and justify German actions, but when properly discounted they are extremely useful. Their accuracy can be tested against other contemporary accounts, some friendly, some not, and when put to the test the German accounts of the war present a reasonably exact, if one-sided, picture of the events.

What can we learn of the Hereros and other tribes from the German accounts? At first glance the answer seems to be disappointingly little, but after a few moments' reflection it becomes clear that they yield a significant store of information concerning the motives, plans, and actions of the tribes. This is so because the German accounts at a bare minimum supply us with the movements of the enemy and his numbers (or at least German estimates of his numbers). To the editors of the German history, the movements of the black men are essentially irrational, animal-like responses to stimuli, but such an inter-

3. There are four major letters of Samuel Maharero: one to Hendrik Witbooi, undated but probably written a month before the outbreak of the rebellion; one to Hermanus van Wyk, also undated but probably written sometime in late 1903; a third to Hendrik Witbooi, dated January 11, 1904; and a fourth to Leutwein, dated March 6, 1904. The first two letters are in the Imperial Colonial Archives in Potsdam and have been published in Horst Drechsler's *Südwestafrika unter Deutscher Kolonialherrschaft* (Berlin, 1966). The other two letters have been published in a slightly shortened form by Theodor Leutwein in *Elf Jahre Gouverneur in Deutsch-Südwestafrika* (Leipzig, 1912). I. Goldblatt presents a translation of the second letter in its entirety in his *History of South West Africa* (Cape Town, 1971); the original of that letter was in the possession of Clemens Kapuo, who was chief of the Hereros in 1969.

pretation, though possible, is suspect for two reasons. First, the few actual documents which we have from the tribal side suggest that the leaders had a clear idea of what they were doing, and furthermore their movements make very good military sense indeed. So we can construct an account of African tactics and strategy which, though admittedly speculative, still conforms to all the known facts and is a good deal more plausible than the stimulus-response theory.

But the documents yield us more than straight military history, for they give us some insight into the motives of the tribal leaders. In recent years Africanist scholars have paid particular attention to events during the period 1885-1914, when African societies began movements of resistance and rebellion directed against European conquest and rule.[4] There are studies of societies in neighboring South Africa and Rhodesia whose immediate preconquest history is similar to that of the Herero tribe and other African societies of Southwest Africa.[5] Somewhat further away, in the German colony of Tanganyika, an extremely important Bantu resistance movement called *maji maji* occurred during the years 1904-1907 and was, as in the Herero case of the same period, violently suppressed by German arms.[6] Therefore, a comparative framework exists in which African responses to German conquest and colonial rule can be assessed in order to shed some light on the Herero War.

These studies have emphasized two phases of African resistance, both of which apply directly to South West Africa. Initially, African societies sought to deal with European coloni-

4. The major theoretical statement that focuses attention on African resistance to European conquest may be found in T.O. Ranger, "Connexions between 'primary resistance' movements and modern mass nationalism in East and Central Africa," *Journal of African History*, Vol. IX, nos. 3-4 (1968), pp. 437-453, Part I, and 631-641, Part II. For comparative examples of resistance movements in West Africa, see M. Crowder, ed., *West African Resistance* (London, 1968).

5. On South Africa, see M. Hunter (Monica Wilson), *Reactions to Conquest* (London, 1936); on Rhodesia, see T.O. Ranger, *Revolt in Southern Rhodesia, 1896-7* (London, 1967).

6. J. Iliffe, "Tanzania Under German and British Rule," in B. Ogot, editor, *Zamani: A Survey of East African History* (Nairobi, new edition, 1974), pp. 295-313.

zation by employing traditional means of warfare or diplomacy. When these strategies failed in the face of overwhelming
European superiority in armaments, African leaders sought to
deal with the *fact* of European occupation in other ways. The
first phase has been called "primary resistance" and the second
phase, after the establishment of European power, "secondary
resistance." The Revolt of the Hereros is clearly revealed as a
movement of secondary resistance in which the call to violent
rebellion was raised. Its leaders developed a more effective ideology of rebellion and made skillful use of their knowledge of
the terrain upon which the rebellion was waged in order to
pursue guerrilla tactics. While they failed to dislodge their
German rulers—just as the *maji maji* rebellion had failed to do
in Tanganyika—it remained clear that the seeds of a new political consciousness had been sown among those who survived
the holocaust of rebellion and its ruthless suppression. One
irony is that the German military leaders in Tanganyika apparently learned from and put to use this new political consciousness bred from the *maji maji* experience, and were able to
recruit a potent guerrilla force from among their former adver-
saries that held out against a major British and South African
army until 1919.[7]

In South West Africa the results were far different. The devastating suppression of the Herero and Hottentot rebels meant
that no German allies were available among them when South
Africa invaded, conquered, and held this colony from 1915 to
the present day. On the other hand, the new political consciousness that developed during the Herero rebellion has made its
appearance in various ways since then, despite the equally
authoritarian South African regime under which the survivors
of that revolt have lived. In 1972 a general strike took place in
South West Africa which included a pronounced element of
Herero leadership. And, in the most recent series of developments, the Hereros have constituted one of the main parties
seeking political independence for the country now named

7. C. Miller, *Battle for the Bundu: The First World War in East Africa*
(New York, 1974).

Namibia. While there is, of course, no direct provable connection between the ideology of rebellion that animated Herero secondary resistance in the first decade of this century and the present aims of Namibia's African nationalists, the same people continue to wage a struggle with the same central purpose: to reassert their control over a land they claim as their own.

The story of the Herero Revolt has the elements of both a past and a continuing story. In the early years of this century a few thousand poorly armed Africans held the world's greatest military power at bay for three years, to succumb only after overwhelming forces were put in the field against them. But the destruction of the Herero tribes on the desert, their suffering in the labor camps, the thousands upon thousands of deaths without purpose or dignity, rob the story of any element of triumph.[8] The end was pure tragedy, unrelieved by any hope for the immediate future. It is not a pleasant story. But the heroism of yesterday's rebels is remembered by today's nationalist leaders as an important chapter in a people's struggle to achieve human dignity in the modern world, and in this sense, it is both timely and worth our attention.

8. "The settler makes history and is conscious of making it. And because he constantly refers to the history of his mother-country, he clearly indicates that he himself is an extension of the mother country. Thus the history which he writes is not the history of the country which he plunders but the history of his own nation in regard to all that she skims off, all that she violates and starves. The immobility to which the native is condemned can only be called in question if the native decides to put an end to the history of colonization—the history of pillage—and to bring into existence the history of the nation—the history of decolonization." Frantz Fanon, *The Wretched of the Earth* (New York, 1963), p. 41.

1
South West Africa: The Land and the People

SOUTH WEST AFRICA even today is a barren and desolate land; it was all the more so seventy years ago when the Hereros rose in revolt against their German masters. A few weeks after the revolt broke out an officer recorded his initial impression upon seeing the coast line for the first time. "Everything looked so dead, so bleak, so deserted," he wrote. "There were no palms, no woods, no trees, no shrubs: only stones, rocks and sand. . . . We gazed at the shore with anxiety and astonishment."[1] The officer's lament illustrates one of the major problems facing the Germans during the revolt: except for a handful of men who had actually been to the colony, almost no other Germans had any idea at all what the country was like. A full year before the fighting erupted, a clear warning was given to anyone who would listen. Curt von François, an old colonial hand who knew South West Africa intimately, predicted that should it be necessary to send an expedition to the South West, the difficulties would be legion. Von Francois sought to dispel the commonly held illusion that a few regulars could quickly handle any number of "half-naked savages." He foresaw that a long

1. M. Bayer, *Mit Hauptquartier in Südwestafrika* (Berlin, 1909), p. 8.

8

and difficult effort would be required to put down a full-scale revolt. The Dutch and English, he noted, had taken two hundred years to break the resistance of the indigenous tribes in the Cape. "And now the most independent of those natives reside in our colony . . . and they are no longer armed only with bows and arrows but now they have modern breech-loading rifles and in the final analysis they respect only power."[2] This sensible advice was ignored, if indeed it was ever read. There is little evidence that the German general staff officers who directed the overall conduct of the campaign, from desks ten thousand miles away from the scene of the action, ever really understood the nature of the fighting, or that they more than dimly perceived that the maxims they had learned in cadet school were useless, or worse, in the type of war that developed in South West Africa.

Geography

Geographical factors in a large measure circumscribed military operations in South West Africa.[3] First among these was the remoteness of the terrain of battle. Virtually all the fighting during the revolt took place on the central plateau, an extensive plain excellent for grazing but far too arid for dry farming. Surrounding this plain on all sides were forbidding deserts which from time immemorial had discouraged all but the most adventurous or the most desperate people from reaching it. Before the Germans annexed South West Africa most people had entered the land either from the northeast, as the Hereros and Ovambos had done, or the southwest, as in the case of the Hottentots. Political considerations, however, prevented the Germans from using either of these well marked routes, for to have done so would have required going through the territory of others—either Portuguese Angola, British Bechuanaland, or

2. Quoted in Kurt Schwabe, *Der Krieg in Deutsch-Südwestafrika* (Berlin, 1907), pp. i-ii.
3. John H. Wellington, *South West Africa and its Human Issues*, has the best general introduction to the geography of South West Africa. Hans Meyer, ed., *Das Deutsche Kolonialreich* (2 vols., Leipzig, 1910), is also useful.

the Cape Colony. Since the Germans wanted to avoid being dependent on others for access to their colony, they were forced to come by sea, the most difficult of all the routes. "How spirited must have been the hearts of those who first dared to establish themselves on so inhospitable a coast," exclaimed a soldier on first seeing it. The seas were often stormy; fogs shrouded the coast for most of the year, and along the whole 800-mile length of the coastline there was only one real harbor, Walvis Bay, and that was a British possession. The Germans were left with two open roadsteads, Swakopmund and Lüderitz Bay. Neither had piers capable of handling ocean-going vessels or safe anchorages. To off-load a ship in either harbor was a time-consuming, costly, and often dangerous procedure.

The problems of getting cargo to the beach, difficult as they were, were minor compared with the awesome task of negotiating the Namib desert. Averaging 75 miles in width, the Namib is a waterless nightmare whose only known vegetation is the *Welwitschia mirabilis*, a scrub plant adapted to survive in conditions where rainfall is under one inch yearly.[4] Until the completion of the railroad from Swakopmund to Windhoek in 1902, the crossing of the Namib was an epic undertaking, and even after the railroad was in operation the difficulties were by no means ended. To save money, the Germans had built a narrow gauge railroad whose track was only 60 centimeters wide. The tiny engines could not pull more than six cars, which held at most five tons of goods each. The condition of the track and roadbed was so precarious that only in exceptional circumstances did the administrators of the line try to send out more than one train a day. As a matter of course, every train that set out on the 238-mile journey carried a repair crew, spare parts, ties, rails, and crushed rock. Schedules meant nothing; almost never did a train complete a journey without at least one major mishap.

Once the Namib was negotiated, the landscape took on a

4. This unique plant was first discovered in 1858 by the explorer Friedrich Martin Josef Welwitsch. Its taproot is up to sixty feet long in a mature plant. On the surface it has two leathery leaves, which are often torn to shreds by the wind.

somewhat more promising appearance, but despite the wide
expanses of grassland and bracing climate, the plateau was an
extremely poor land. There were a few scattered trees, but they
produced no usable lumber. Outside the immediate vicinity of
the towns there was no cultivated land. And most important of
all, water was a luxury. Although the more favored areas in the
central part of the plateau received an average annual rainfall
of close to 15 inches a year, that figure alone is misleading, in
view of two others: all the rain was concentrated in a five-
month period from December to April; and in one year out of
four the annual rainfall fell off by a quarter, and in one year out
of seven it was only half the normal. Still, by exploiting the
water resources to the utmost the natives in the favored areas
managed to maintain sizable herds of cattle. In the southern
parts of the colony where the rainfall rarely exceeded ten inches
a year, the stands of grass were much sparser than in the north
and only sheep and goats could be raised there. In 1904 the
population density for the whole colony was not much more
than one person per square mile, and even that number put a
clear strain on the resources of the land.

In all of South West Africa there are no perennial rivers save
those on the northern and southern boundaries. The few rivers
on the plateau are classed as either "periodic" or "episodic."

TABLE 1
Average Annual Rainfall

Station	Position	Altitude (meters)	Average annual rainfall (millimeters)
Warmbad	28°27′S.,18°44′E.	750	86
Keetmanshoop	26°35′S.,18°08′E.	1004	133
Gibeon	25°08′S.,17°45′E.	1059	174
Windhoek	22°34′S.,17°06′E.	1728	363
Omaruru	21°25′S.,15°56′E.	1211	306

SOURCE: John H. Wellington, *South West Africa and Its Human Issues*
(Oxford, 1967), p. 36.

The most important of the periodic rivers, the Swakop, flowed twenty times a year on the average, with each flow lasting three to four days. At the other end of the scale were the episodic rivers, some of which remained dry for decades. Though there was little flowing water in South West Africa and by most standards the land was near desert, still there was water for those who knew how to find it. During the dry season, water could be found either in the beds of the periodic rivers, ten to thirty feet below the surface, or in the vleys—depressions with clay or chalk bottoms in which rain water was trapped during the rainy season. Some vleys would retain water for several months, but by the end of the yearly drought they were inevitably dry. The quality of the underground water was unpredictable: sometimes it was murky and brackish, sometimes sweet and pure. In the three years before the outbreak of the rebellion there was a general drought in all of South West Africa: in the north the annual rainfall was only about 70 percent of normal and in the south less than half. In 1904 and 1905, however, the rainfall was well above normal. The Hereros, who knew the land intimately, had an uncanny knack for finding water even in the driest times, but the Germans, totally inexperienced as most of them were, were completely dependent on known waterholes. Only on rare occasions does one hear of Germans digging wells or locating vleys. "In the interior there were, to be sure, numerous waterholes," wrote one of the German commanders, von Deimling, "but they were known to the natives and not to us. Henrik Witbooi can live with his people for months on end out on the Kalahari desert and yet our maps showed this area to be completely waterless."

If the lack of water was the greatest single problem facing the German military commanders in their attempts to carry on warfare on the plateau, the ubiquitous thorn bushes were a close second.[5] Most of the thorn bushes were acacias; some, like the sweet thorn (*Acacia karroo*), had vicious thorns two to three inches long. So thick were the thorn bushes in many parts of

5. There are more than forty species of *acacia* (*Leguminosae*) in southern Africa. In South West Africa, they are particularly plentiful in Hereroland.

Hereroland that they became a major obstacle to military activity. "These damned thorn bushes imprison us," wrote a soldier during the first campaign. "They choke us, rob us of light and air. One feels as if one were in a sack, unable to move freely or to make a vigorous decision. One can only lie in anger and rage and wait."[6] Men who became entangled in thorn thickets often sustained painful injuries before they could free themselves. Like the shortage of water the thorns were a fact of life in South West Africa. The African herdsmen and hunters had learned to adapt to them and even used them to their advantage, but the Germans found them a constant vexation.

The harshness of this environment had been but little mitigated by the art of man. In the whole of the plateau there were no roads worthy of the name. The trails that did exist were, in most places, barely marked paths through heavy sand into which the wheels of wagons often sunk a foot or more. Twenty, sometimes even forty, oxen were needed to pull an average wagon. To add to their difficulties, the Germans had not mapped most of the land. Almost no food was grown outside the immediate vicinity of the towns. It followed, then, that the logistical problems of maintaining a sizable force on the plateau were formidable, and to carry on large-scale military operations strained even the resources and the ingenuity of the German army.

Given the resources of a modern state and the will to use them, however, the harsh realities of the geography of South West Africa did not pose insurmountable obstacles to carrying on war there. Indeed, more than a few German officers found the challenges of fighting in South West Africa a welcome diversion from the tedium of peacetime service. Still, it is sobering to contemplate the amount of blood and treasure, on both sides, that the Germans were willing to expend in order to gain absolute control over that unappealing corner of the earth. To most Germans, the slaughter of tens of thousands of Africans, the loss of two thousand of their own soldiers, and the expenditure of a half-billion marks did not seem too high a price to pay for dominion over South West Africa.

6. Bayer, *Mit Hauptquartier*, p. 51.

The Indigenous Societies of South West Africa

The indigenous societies of South West Africa are related to two main ethno-linguistic stocks: the Bantu-speaking groups of the north and central regions, and the Khoisan-derived peoples of the southern and more arid districts. Within these broad categories many small-scale kinship groupings and several larger units, termed tribes, can be identified.

The Bantu tribes, though closely related linguistically, are culturally separated into two groups, the Ovambo and the Herero. The Ovambo were agriculturalists who lived along the northern border of the colony among the numerous water-courses that led into the Etosha Pan.[7] By skillful exploitation of their water supply the Ovambo were able to extract a tolerable living from their land. Their principal crop was millet, which was supplemented by Kaffir corn, beans, pumpkins, melons, and peanuts. In addition to farming, the Ovambos kept a few domestic animals and gathered a variety of wild fruits and berries. Because the women of the tribe did most of the work in the fields, the men were free to devote their energies to cultivating the arts of war. Well armed with an impressive array of primitive weapons, the Ovambo warriors discouraged even the peaceful explorer from passing through their land. A handful of missionaries labored manfully in these barren fields, but after twenty years of work they could claim less than one convert a year. Even the Germans, who claimed sovereignty over the land, left the Ovambos to their own devices, reckoning that the cost of imposing effective rule over them would not be worth the effort. In the early days of their rule the Germans built a fort at Namutoni on the eastern edge of the Etosha Pan, and for all practical purposes that fort marked the northern

7. For anthropological information, see C. H. L. Hahn, "The Ovambo," in *Native Tribes of South West Africa* (Cape Town, 1928). This volume contains four other essays: one by L. Fourie, "The Bushmen of South West Africa," and three by H. Vedder—"The Nama," "The Berg Damara," and "The Herero." The Etosha Pan is a salt lake covering 2300 square miles. It is fed by numerous rivers but most of their water is lost by evaporation. At the present time it is a game reserve, and around its shores are some of the last great herds of big game to be found in South West Africa.

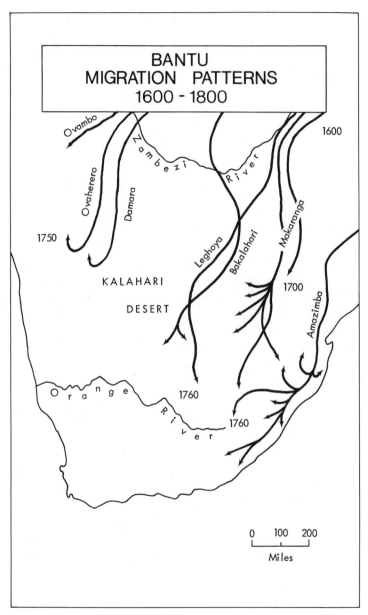

BANTU
MIGRATION PATTERNS
1600 - 1800

Ovambo

Zambezi

River

1600

Ovaherero

Damara

1750

Leghoya

Bakalahari

Makaranga

1700

Amazimba

KALAHARI

DESERT

Orange

River

1760

1760

0   100   200

Miles

Map 1

limit of their power. Though at the time of the revolt the Ovambos accounted for almost half of the total population of South West Africa, they played no role in the great events of 1904-1907.

The Herero, on the other hand, were the instigators of the revolt and the people on whom the wrath of the Germans fell most heavily.[8] Although individual Hereros survived the ordeal, the tribe as such perished. Unlike the Ovambos, the Hereros were a pastoral people, ignorant of the art of metallurgy and contemptuous of agriculture, which they left to their serfs. Physically, the Hereros were so strikingly handsome that they greatly impressed early travelers. "The Damara [the Hottentot name for Hereros, meaning simply black man], speaking generally, are an exceedingly fine race of men," wrote the Swedish explorer Charles John Andersson in 1850. "Indeed, it is by no means unusual to meet with individuals six feet and some inches in height, and symmetrically proportioned withal. Their features are, besides, good and regular; and many might serve as perfect models of the human figure. Their air and carriage, moreover, is very graceful and expressive."[9] When Andersson got to know the Hereros rather more intimately, this favorable impression waned. High on the list of things that offended his Victorian sensibilities was the problem of personal hygiene. "Both sexes are exceedingly filthy in their habits. Dirt often accumulates to such a degree on their persons, as to make the colour of their skin totally indistinguishable; while, to complete the disguise, they smear themselves with a profusion of red ochre and grease. Hence the exhalation hovering about them is disgusting in the extreme."[10] Besides being dirty, Europeans accused the Hereros of being cruel, deceitful, and untrustworthy. The first charge is no doubt true, although in this regard the Germans ran them a close second; as for the other charges the verdict must be "not proven," but more of that later.

    8. See H. Vedder, "The Herreros," in *Native Tribes.*
    9. Charles Andersson, *Lake Ngami, or Exploration and Discovery during Four Years Wanderings in the Wilds of South-Western Africa* (London, 1956), p. 49.
    10. *Ibid.*, p. 50.

To understand the culture of the Herero one must understand the role that cattle played in every aspect of the lives of
these people. The Herero language, for example, which was
vocabulary-poor in most areas, contains more than a thousand
words for the colors and markings of cattle. According to Herero myths, the creator gave them the cow and the bull, while
the rest of mankind had to be satisfied with lesser gifts. The
Herero's love for his cattle was legendary. As one Herero explained to a German: "Everyone is greedy. The European is
devoted to dead metals. We are more intelligent, we get our joy
out of living creatures."[11] And joy it was. "The Herero loved his
cattle," wrote a German official, "and for their sake no labor was
too great. For long hours beneath the scorching sun the Herero
would draw water, bucket by bucket, from the waterholes for
the animals to drink. For days and weeks he would persevere
despite terrible hardships in search of one lost or strayed ani-
mal. His whole object in life was the increase and preservation
of his herds which in the favorable climate and environment of
Hereroland throve wonderfully."[12] So much did the Herero
love his animals that he rarely slaughtered them. The basis of
his diet was sour milk mixed with blood drawn from his cattle
and the wild fruits and berries that he found in the bush. As
long as the Herero had plenty of pasture and his herds were safe
from cattle thieves he was content to live in peace; but when his
cattle were threatened, the peaceful Herero became a formidable
warrior.

When the Germans first came in contact with them, the
Hereros were emerging politically from a purely tribal state
into what German Marxist writers call Nomadic Early Feudalism (Nomadenfrühfeudalismus). Heinrich Loth, in his study of
the missions in South West Africa, defines this cumbersome
term in the following way.

> The process of social differentiation had advanced so far . . . that
> the outlines of a class structure were already beginning to ap-
> pear. The basis of this structure was the possession of cattle,

11. Felix Meyer, *Wirtschaft und Recht der Herero* (Berlin, 1905), pp.
18-19. Quoted in Wellington, *South West Africa*, p. 148.
12. J. Irle, *Die Herero* (Gütersloh, 1906), p. 121.

which were the principal means of production in private hands.
. . . [Land, it should be noted, was held communally.] An
inclination towards group ownership is a distinctive feature of
Nomadic Feudalism. Property rights to cattle were protected by
a well organized juridical system. There were some Hereros who
owned several hundred head of cattle while the richest of them
possessed up to 10,000 head of cattle, sheep, and goats. In contrast to this class of rich cattle-owners stood the simple folk who
might possess a few animals or perhaps none at all. The poor
were dominated by the rich and worked for them as herdsmen. In
social development the Herero . . . were in a transitional stage on
their way to Nomadic Feudalism. In the system of dependent
relations we can recognize clear traces of the feudal exploitative
system, although not based on land but rather on the possession
of cattle.[13]

The political organization of the Hereros is a good deal more
complicated than Loth is willing to admit. Before about 1870—
that is, before the influence of the whites became the determin-
ing factor—the Hereros' socio-political organization was a
complex system of paternal and maternal groupings. The tribe
was divided into about 20 different "oruzo" or paternal derivation groups. Each oruzo was headed by a chief who normally,
but not always, acquired his position through inheritance. The
oruzo held in trust a number of sacred cattle which were inalienable and which were only used for sacrifice. The members
of an oruzo lived together in a werft (village), which was a circle
of pontoks (mud and dung thatched huts). The chief, as the
religious leader of the oruzo, lived in the biggest pontok (although it actually belonged to his wife); in the other pontoks
were his concubines, married sons, unmarried children, and
other dependents. Within the circle of pontoks was the kraal
where the calves were kept. In the center of the werft was a
sacred fire (okuruuo), the tending of which was one of the main
duties of the chief. If the werft became too large, the chief would
permit one of the young men and his dependents to found a
new werft. The inhabitants of the new werft, however, remained dependent on their original chief. Parallel to the oruzo

13. Heinrich Loth, *Die Christliche Mission in Südwestafrika* (Berlin, 1963), pp. 23-24.

groups were the "eanda" groups, which were maternal. As opposed to the oruzo cattle which were sacred and inalienable, the cattle of the eanda could be used for paying debts and were often lent out to poorer members of the group. Whereas the members of the oruzo group normally lived together, those of the eanda were forbidden to live in the same werft. All land was held to be common property of the tribe and could not be alienated except for some temporary purpose.

Between 1870 and 1904 this traditional system began to disintegrate. The Germans created Samuel Maharero as the paramount chief of the tribe although no such office existed in traditional Herero culture. As a Christian, Samuel could not tend the sacred fire, although that was one of the primary functions of the chief. As the possibility of selling cattle for cash expanded, some Hereros began to be transformed from tribesmen into cattle ranchers. Some social differentiation began to become evident between the poor "field Hereros" who owned few or no cattle and were thus obliged to work, and the richer chiefs who had large herds. Herero males traditionally did no "work" except that connected with their own cattle. After the uprising the Germans extinguished all the sacred fires and confiscated all the cattle, so that the whole traditional basis of Herero cooperative life, which was already beginning to decay by 1904, collapsed completely and the Hereros became hired herdsmen on white men's ranches. "Now there were only Herero laborers, for the Herero nation existed no longer, and strict, but just laws regulated natives' affairs."[14]

In 1903 the Herero nation was divided into nine tribes. The largest of these was centered around the town of Okahandja and was estimated to have 23,000 members living in some 150 villages. At the time of the uprising the leader of the Okahandja Hereros was Samuel Maharero, and by virtue of the size of his tribe and his personal wealth, he had a claim to be the leader of all the Hereros, a claim which the Germans did everything to foster. To the west of Okahandja were two other tribes: one located in the vicinity of Omaruru under Chief Manasse, and

14. *Native Tribes*, p. 162.

the other at Otijimbingwe under Chief Zacharias. In the north around Mount Waterberg lived the people of Chief Kambazeni. In the east there were five small tribes led by Nikodemus, Tjetjo, Mambo, Ombondju, and Kakimena. The power of a Herero chief was in large measure determined by the number of cattle he owned: rich chiefs attracted many followers and poor chiefs had but few. But even the richest chief was no more than a *primus inter pares*, for all of the cattle-owners in the tribe claimed a share in making all decisions. There was no intra-tribal authority as such, although the chiefs did confer from time to time on matters of common interest.

Were the Hereros "barbarians" in the worst sense of the word? Naturally, it is impossible to give an unqualified answer to such a question, but one can offer a few suggestions. On the affirmative side, one can point out that the Hereros did carry on warfare with considerable and often gratuitous cruelty. The flavor of their war-making can be gathered from the following description of the treatment meted out to a band of Hottentots caught stealing cattle. "Returning from Hornkranz we came across a few Hottentots whom of course we killed. I myself helped to kill one of them. First we cut off his ears saying to him, 'You will never again hear Damara cattle lowing.' Then we cut off his nose saying, 'Never again shall you smell Damara oxen.' And then we cut off his lips, saying, 'You shall never again taste Damara oxen.' And then finally we cut his throat."[15] This is not an isolated horror story, for cruelty undoubtedly played an integral part in the life of the Herero, but there is another side to the story. Despite the terrible cruelty the Herero exercised on occasion, they did not live in a Hobbesian night-mare, the war of all against all. The Hereros had a reasonably well-developed sense of orderly international relations and they regulated their affairs with other tribes on the basis of treaties. On balance, the Hereros kept their treaties about as consistently as European nations did; that is to say, they carried out the provisions of a treaty if they found it to their own interest. The Herero system of law, though primitive by European standards,

15. Wellington, *South West Africa*, p. 148.

was not without an elementary sense of equity and justice. Take, for example, the following description of a Herero legal proceeding written in the mid-nineteenth century by a missionary.

The court proceeding took place in the middle of a village under a shady thorn tree. The accused was a young man about thirty who had forcibly turned out his aged father that morning. On order of the chief, to whom the unfortunate old man had made a complaint, the guilty party together with the members of his family who had anything to do with the expulsion, had to leave the area at once and seek a new home in the mountains on the other side of the Omaruru River. Instead of obeying these orders, the criminal rashly appeared soon again with a loaded gun. Before he could make use of the weapon, he was seized by three strong men who dragged him by main force to a hillock where the chief dwelt. The chief had the court convened at once with a sub-chief presiding since he was too ill to appear in person. The news spread like wildfire through the village and from every nook and cranny the curious hastened to the deliberation which took place under the aforementioned tree. Even the lovely green gardens on the Omaruru, where normally brisk activity rules, were soon deserted as all came to the trial. The session was open to all with the exception of women. The high tribunal, consisting of the sub-chief who presided, two judges, and three jurors, sat on the ground as did all the others. Before them stood the accused. The trial began. "Why have you not left this place?" demanded the judge. "I will not leave," answered the accused defiantly. There followed a short debate between the judge and the jurors. The sub-chief ordered quiet and said: "Because you have not obeyed, you will now receive twenty-five lashes."[16]

Perhaps this is not the standard of justice one would expect in an English courtroom of the day, but surely it is not much different from that being meted out in the American west. Nineteenth-century explorers and travelers described in great detail the culture of the Hereros, including what they considered the barbarous elements, but they did not write the Hereros off as unregenerate savages. Quite the contrary, they argued that the introduction of missionaries, the opening of the land to

16. See H. Vedder, *South West Africa in Early Times* (Oxford, 1938), pp. 227ff, for most complete analysis of native systems of justice.

world trade, and the establishment of hospitals and schools would soon bring the barbarism to an end. Modern colonial apologists, particularly South Africans, have none of the broad tolerance of the early visitors; they paint a picture of undifferentiated savagery of life in South West Africa before the coming of the white man, in contrast to the present rule of law and order. "Danger to life, and terror, came from within the group," wrote a South African in 1963. "The chief's power was absolute. A nod from him was sufficient to sentence a man to any kind of death his executioners chose to inflict. . . . The punishment of sorcerers and witches was prescribed. Sticks were placed on either side of the sorcerer's head and secured back and front with thongs. The thongs were twisted till the skull cracked and the eyeballs shot out of their sockets."[17] The account is probably accurate, but it is useful to remember that the last witch was hanged in England in 1753. On balance, it seems not unreasonable to conclude that while the Hereros were certainly not "happy savages" living in a demi-paradise before the coming of the white men, neither were they subhuman monsters with an unquenchable lust for the blood of their fellow men.

To the south of the Hereros lived four Khoisan peoples: the Hottentots (or Namas), the Saan, the Bushmen, and the Orlams.[18] Though culturally quite distinct, these four tribes spoke related languages and shared common physical characteristics. The Khoisan have a yellowish skin tone and are diminutive in stature—the males rarely exceed 4'6" in height—in contrast to the black-skinned, tall Hereros. The most striking peculiarity of the Khoisan is their language, which contains a number of clicking sounds. So bizarre did the speech of these people sound to early travelers that they wondered if the strange chirping creatures they encountered were part of the family of man. For many centuries the most primitive of the Khoisan people, the Bushmen, were the only inhabitants of the plateau of South West Africa. Then in about 1600 a second Khoisan people, the Saan, trekked into the plateau. Like the Bushmen, the Saan

17. Alexander Stewart, *The Sacred Trust* (Johannesburg, 1962), p. 9.
18. See Isaac Shapera, *The Khoisan Peoples of South Africa: Bushmen and Hottentots* (London, 1930).

were hunters and gatherers, and since the land was well stocked with game, the two peoples lived peacefully together. About a hundred years later (c. 1700) the Namas or Hottentots began to enter South West Africa. Racially and linguistically they were closely related to the Saan and more remotely to the Bushmen, but culturally the Namas were considerably advanced over the two tribes that had preceded them into the land north of the Orange River. Besides being pastoralists rather than hunters and gatherers, the Namas also had some knowledge of the use of iron and had evolved a relatively complicated political organization. As they spread north in search of better pasture they drove the Saan and Bushmen out of the most favored areas onto the fringes of the desert. During the course of the eighteenth century eight separate tribes of Namas crossed the Orange. Six of these tribes formed a loose federation under the leadership of the Red Nation tribe, while the two tribes which remained independent were the Bondelzwarts of Warmbad and the Topnaars of Zessfontein. The federated tribes and their home areas are as follows:

Tribe	Area
Khauben (Red Nation) So named because of the reddish tint to their skin	Hoachanas
Franschmannsche Hottentots	Gochas
Veldschoendragers (Wearers of veld shoes)	To the east of the Karras Hills
Zwartboois (Black boys)	Fransfontein
Groot-doden (Great deaths)	Hornkranz
Kara-oan	Fish River Canyon

The largest of these eight tribes did not have more than 3000 members, and the average was much below that figure. Whereas the first white travelers were wont to describe the Hereros as the "natural nobility" of the area, they generally dismissed the Namas as shiftless, lazy, and cruel. "In all the attacks of the Namas," wrote one observer, "the most atrocious barbarities were committed. The men were unmercifully shot down; the hands and feet of the women lopped off; the bowels of the children ripped up, etc., and all this to satisfy a savage thirst for blood."[19]

In the first decades of the nineteenth century, after the Namas were well established in South West Africa, another group of immigrants called Orlams crossed into the region north of the Orange. The exact significance of the word "Orlam" is disputed, but this much is clear: the Orlams were detribalized Namas who had lived for several generations in close proximity to the Dutch at the Cape—in some cases as bonded servants, in some cases as slaves. From their masters the Orlams had picked up a smattering of the Dutch language, a rather peculiar form of the Dutch Reformed religion, and a good many skills including the use of firearms. In many cases the Orlams carried some Dutch blood in their veins, but it is important to note that such unions when they did occur were not recognized by the Dutch. Just beyond the fringe of the civilized area of the Cape, small bands of Orlams carved out a precarious existence, sometimes as nomadic herdsmen, sometimes as outlaws, usually as both. Their numbers were periodically strengthened by the addition of fugitives from the Cape. In the first years of the nineteenth century a band of Orlams requested permission from the Red Nation to cross the Orange and thus escape completely from the authority of the government at the Cape. The Red Nation granted permission and eventually five tribes of Orlams came into South West Africa. These five tribes were the Khowesin or Queen Bees under Kido Witbooi, later to be known as the Witboois; the people of Amraal (the admiral); the Bereseba Hottentots; the Bethanie Hottentots; and the Aicha-Ain or Angry Tribe, who became known later as the Afrikanders, after their leader. Having both guns and horses, the Orlams were at first militarily superior to all the other peoples in South West Africa, but by the middle of the century this initial advantage

19. Almost all travelers had a similar view of the Hottentots. See in particular Andersson, *Lake Ngami*, pp. 322ff.

disappeared as German traders introduced guns to all the peoples of the land.

Two other peoples must be mentioned in this survey of the inhabitants of South West Africa, the Berg Damaras and the Basters. Most of the Berg Damaras were serfs of the Hottentots and the Hereros. Where they came from or how they happened to be a subject race is unclear, but most authorities believe that they must have been conquered and enslaved by the Hottentots many centuries earlier. The Berg Damaras speak the Nama tongue, though not very well, which suggests that it is not their own language. Those Berg Damaras who were not held in bondage lived as hunters and gatherers in the mountainous regions of the land, hence their name, Berg Damaras or "mountain blacks." The Basters were a half-caste people like the Orlams, but unlike them they stemmed from legally recognized and religiously consecrated unions between Dutch men and Hottentot women. The Basters spoke Dutch and proudly carried Dutch names such as van der Byl, Cloete, Vries, and van Wyk. For several generations these people had lived quietly in the region just to the south of the Orange River, then in 1865 the Cape government decreed that all settlers in marginal areas would be obliged to prove title to the lands which they occupied or get out. The Basters, fearing the loss of their lands, trekked into Namaland in 1870 and settled in the vicinity of Reheboth. During the uprising the Basters remained loyal to the Germans and were rewarded by being permitted to retain their lands. In 1915 the Basters again chose the winning side, this time supporting the invaders from the Union of South Africa. Their foresight was again rewarded and to this day they are permitted to live much as they did in 1870.

In 1904 there were three major tribal groupings and some forty different tribes in South West Africa. The agrarian Ovambos were divided into fifteen tribes; the Hereros into nine; and the Hottentots into thirteen (if one includes the Basters and Orlams with the Hottentots). Interspersed among these forty major tribes were small groups of Bushmen, Saan, and Berg Damaras in addition to the white settlers.

African Population Statistics

The British Commissioner, William Coates Palgrave, in a report of 1877, estimated the South West African indigenous population as follows:

Ovambos	98,000
Hereros	85,000
Berg Damaras	30,000
Hottentots	18,350
Basters	1,500
Bushmen	3,000
Total	235,850

In his book, German Governor Leutwein set the population for 1894 as follows:

Ovambos	100,000
Hereros	80,000
Hottentots	20,000
Basters	4,000
Bushmen & Berg Damaras	40,000
Total	244,000

In the second edition of *Mit Schwert und Pflug* (published in 1904), Captain Kurt Schwabe of the German Army, while remarking that a correct estimate of the Berg Damara and Bushmen population was impossible, presented the following figures in regard to the other tribes:

Ovambos	100,000-150,000
Hereros	80,000
Hottentots	20,000
Basters	4,000

A major problem in the historical treatment of widely dispersed kin-based societies is the use of accurate terminology to identify individual units. From the ethno-linguistic perspective, the groups referred to here belong either to the Bantu or Khoi main language families. However, each small group uses its own identifying terminology based not on language classification (a European analytical construct), but rather on case-specific historical material: for example, a group may be named after a commonly recognized putative ancestor; or it may take

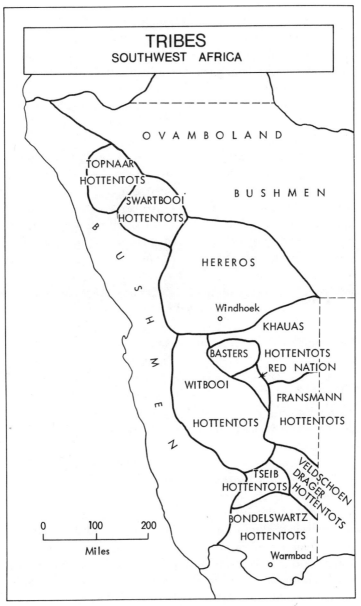

TRIBES
SOUTHWEST AFRICA

O V A M B O L A N D

TOPNAAR
HOTTENTOTS

SWARTBOOI
HOTTENTOTS

B U S H M E N

B U S H M E N

HEREROS

Windhoek

KHAUAS

BASTERS

HOTTENTOTS
RED NATION

WITBOOI

FRANSMANN

HOTTENTOTS

HOTTENTOTS

TSEIB
HOTTENTOTS

VELDSCHOEN
DRAGER
HOTTENTOTS

BONDELSWARTZ

HOTTENTOTS

Warmbad

0   100   200

Miles

Map 2

its name from some natural or geographic feature with which the group is associated. More common still, insofar as the ethnographic literature is concerned, is the use of proper nomenclature provided by one group to identify a neighbor: thus, the South African Dutch-speakers called the Khoi subgroup of cattle-keepers whom they encountered in the Western Cape by the name Hottentot, which seemed to them an approximation of the click sounds so uniquely a feature of all Khoisan speech.

As Europeans began to enter Southwest Africa in the early nineteenth century, they adopted and developed a general set of ethno-linguistic categories, "tribal" names, and often derogatory nicknames that drew on all these sources; that is to say, the proper or "tribal" nomenclature used to describe the indigenous societies of South West Africa is itself the product of an historical etymology that evolved throughout the nineteenth century and became fixed only with the establishment of formal European colonial rule. Therefore, the assignment of a given individual to one or another "tribe" must take account of this process if error is to be avoided in the use of terms. Since the focal period of this study is the period nearly thirty years after the establishment of formal German colonial rule in South West Africa, it is most convenient to use the terminology of the German authorities in referring to the individual groups of indigenous peoples treated in the narrative. In this sense, such major groupings as the Herero, Hottentot, and Ovambo are identifiable groups to which the more inclusive term *tribe* will be applied.

A more vexatious terminological problem is raised by the use of the term *native*. Its root meaning, of course, derives from the notion of being "indigenous," or belonging to a place or group by virtue of birth within a specific place or society. But its clear connotation in the history of the contacts established between Africans and Europeans involves both a racial and a cultural set of distinctions. Natives, to all the Europeans who came to rule African populations, were regarded not only as indigenous populations but also as culturally inferior. The easiest way to identify them was by reference to perceived racial differences. Thus, in the South West African case after the establishment of

German rule, a person was referred to as a native if he or she were (a) either non-European or of mixed racial ancestry (the Basters); (b) a member of a recognized tribe; (c) considered to belong to the colony's *subject* populations (that is, lacking recourse to European legal protection but governed instead by "native custom and law"). Thus the term "native" is more than just the reflection of European ethnocentricity: by the time of the Herero Rebellion, "natives" constituted a legal and actual category of the population of the Germany colony; they were the ruled—or subject—majority of the population.

The problem of terminology will be met in the following ways in this study. Where there is no question, the proper (or tribal) terminology—Herero, Hottentot, or Ovambo—will be used. Where the references in German documentation are no more specific than to those peoples whom they, the rulers, have assigned to subject status, the term "native" will be left to stand with the connotative and denotative meanings it had in the period covered by our story.

2

South West Africa
Before the Uprising

THE WHITE MAN did not bring war to South West Africa. The cycle of tribal wars began more than a decade before the first traders and missionaries arrived and fifty years before the Germans proclaimed their protectorate. The wars that were fought before German arrival had the same characteristics as those which had spread like wildfire through the coastal and high Veld regions of South Africa in the first third of the nineteenth century.[1] Those wars, called by the term *difaquane* ("the time of troubles, or wandering"), were ignited by Shaka's Zulu in Natal and spread rapidly to the Sotho-Tswana Bantu populations of the interior districts. They were wars in which a new and devastatingly effective tactical scheme of unconditional conquest came to replace the earlier forms of conflict represented by cattle-raiding. The main problem that set the scene for the outbreak of the *difaquane* was competition for the scarce resource of grazing land.[2] By the 1830's Zulu-derived armies had swept north of the Limpopo river two thousand miles (to the southern Lakes districts) and also westward through the semi-

1. L. M. Thompson, "Co-operation and Conflict: The High Veld," Chapter IX in M. Wilson and L. M. Thompson, eds., *The Oxford History of South Africa*, Vol. I (Oxford, 1969), pp. 391-405, is a masterful interpretive synthesis of this important period in Southern African Bantu history.
2. *Ibid.*, pp. 391-394.

arid grassland of the Northern Cape and Bechuanaland. While the conflicts that burst out between the tribes of South West Africa were not specifically related to the Zulu *difaquane*, they shared the same basic inspiration—competition for grazing land—and general features: that is, they became conflicts in which the aim of warriors was to annihilate the opposition and seize their lands.[3]

The Germans, when they arrived in the midst of these tribal conflicts, finally brought an end to this new and enormously destructive phase of African warfare. The peace that the Germans established was, to be sure, the peace of a graveyard, but for all that it did create the one absolutely necessary precondition for the development of any civilized society, a measure of domestic tranquility. German rule also brought forced labor, the rhino whip, and racial degradation. Whether this was too high a price to pay for peace is problematical.

The Tribal Wars

The year 1830 marks the beginning of tribal war in South West Africa. Prior to that time the various peoples had lived together there in comparative peace. Occasional skirmishes were certainly not unknown, but they never approached the scale of serious warfare. The basis of this international amity was not far to seek, for until the nineteenth century the population was so slight that there was plenty of land and plenty of game for all. The Namas freely granted permission to immigrants to enter their lands—a fact which strongly suggests that in those early days they had no anxiety about overpopulation. The Hereros, too, lived for nearly two centuries in South West Africa without encroaching upon the lands of their neighbors. The doyen of South West African historians, Heinrich Vedder, has recorded the following description of life before the beginning of the tribal wars, given to him by an aged Herero whose memory stretched far back into the past:

3. Vedder, *South West Africa in Early Times* (Oxford, 1938), pp. 169-177.

Have not the Hereros been cattle-breeders ever since God created them? As a cattle-breeder, does not one live in the selfsame way? One treks with the herd wherever water and grazing are to be found and, in the meantime, the cattle increase. Sometimes they are stolen by our enemies; sometimes no thefts take place for years at a time. That is the life of a Herero; that was the life my great-grandfather lived, that was the life my grandfather lived, and my father lived it too. When we live exactly the same way there is not much to be told. Some people are surprised that we have so little to tell about our leaving the Kaokoveld, but I am not a bit surprised about it. [The Hereros left the Kaokoveld and trekked into Hereroland in the middle of the eighteenth century]. Was not the whole land actually one land? The people of old trekked about just where they pleased. Whenever water and grazing were plentiful they stayed for some considerable time, but when these were scarce they soon trekked away. They, therefore, drove their cattle southward out of the Kaokoveld and, when it did not suit them anymore, they often trekked back to the Kaokoveld again. When it was no longer convenient for them to stay there, they came back into Hereroland until, at last, they stayed here for good. So it never really occurred to the old folk that anything great had occurred when they left the Kaokoveld and sought new pastures here. This country had no owners then, unless we are to regard the Bergdamas and the Bushmen, who live in the veld like wild animals, as owners.[4]

The picture the old man gives conforms reasonably well with what we know about the prehistory of South West Africa; it was by no means a garden of Eden, but at least it was a land free from the curse of war.

Shortly after 1800 two new factors appeared in South West Africa, and they ultimately shattered the peace. About 1810 the first white hunters began crossing the Orange River in search of ivory. Because the hunters' only interest was in the ivory and the Namas only wanted the meat, the two were willing to cooperate. The introduction of guns, however, upset the delicate ecological balance which up to that time had kept the numbers of men and the herds of wild animals in a reasonable relationship with one another. Within a generation the once vast herds of elephants were seriously depleted, while at the same time the Nama population increased rapidly due to the

4. *Ibid.*, p. 145.

expanding supply of food. As long as the Namas had been armed only with neolithic weapons their survival in South West Africa was assured, but as soon as they acquired modern weapons even their meagre numbers strained the resources of the land.

At the same time that the hunters began to cross the Orange River in search of ivory the Orlam tribes also began to drift into South West Africa. Between 1815 and 1830 five groups of Orlams received permission from the Red Nation to settle in their lands. In contrast to the Namas and Hereros, who were primarily pacific and fought only when provoked, the Orlams were fighters who only reluctantly pursued a peaceful way of life. Their mere presence in South West Africa had an unsettling effect, because they were well-armed, wild, unruly, and spoiling for a fight. Then in 1829-1830 a great drought gripped the land. The Hereros, in an effort to find pasture for their cattle, began to range further and further to the south. The Namas, too weak to stop them, turned in desperation to the Orlams and asked the strongest of their leaders, Jonker Afrikander, to lead them in driving the Hereros back to the north. Jonker, who had visions of dominating all South West Africa, took up arms at once and in so doing became de facto leader of all the Namas. In 1836 an explorer described him as follows:

> He was a little, modest looking man, with the usual Namaqua features, as to high cheek bones, narrow eyes, and prominent lips, but his nose was slightly inclined to aquiline. He had nothing in his outward manner to denote the bold and intrepid warrior who had beaten the formidable tribe of Kamaka Damap, and thus saved the Namaquas of the Upper Fish River from annihilation. But Aramap [Jonker], like other great Commanders, though short, is distinguished by a daring mind, by good judgment, and by very active habits.[5]

The first war, if one could call it that, dragged on for twelve years (1830-1842), during which time Jonker consistently maintained the initiative. For the most part there was no large-scale fighting, and the military operations were little more than

---

5. Sir James Alexander, *An Expedition of Discovery into the Interior of Africa* (2 vols., London, 1838), II, 154-155.

cattle-stealing raids. In 1842 a peace was signed between the
Hereros and the Orlams which brought the desultory fighting
to a temporary end. So far as one can judge from the scanty
records available, this first war was neither very bloody nor very
destructive.

Peace, it turned out, was ruinous for Jonker. Once the fighting stopped more and more merchants began to congregate at
his camp, offering for sale guns, ammunition, alcohol, and the
other benefits of advanced civilization. Jonker's appetite for the
white man's wares was considerably greater than his ability to
pay, and before long he was deeply in debt to a trader named
Morris. In the halcyon days of war Jonker had always had
plenty of cattle with which to pay his debts, but peace dried up
his source of supply. Morris helpfully suggested that Jonker
could easily refill his kraals by the simple expedient of stealing
a few Herero cattle. Jonker succumbed to the temptation; the
Hereros retaliated and in 1846, after only four years of peace,
the second war had begun. From all indications this second
war, which also lasted twelve years (1846-1858), was much
bloodier than the first, and the principal victims were the
Hereros, who still lacked firearms. In 1856 at a conference of
missionaries it was reported: "The Herero race has so far as we
know ceased to exist. There are only individuals left, without
any kind of link between them, who wander about in a state of
great misery."[6] A traveler through Namaland reported: "they
[the Namas] do not hesitate to thrash a poor wretch with a
sjambok until the skin breaks with every blow, exposing raw
flesh, and sometimes indeed the place of chastisement is covered
with blood, just as if a sheep had been slaughtered there."[7]
Though the reports of the demise of the Herero tribe were
somewhat exaggerated, the numbers of Hereros who died during the twelve years must have been considerable.

The war finally came to an end in 1858, when Jonker bowed
to the pressure exerted on him both by the missionaries and by
his Nama allies. The interest of the Namas in ending the

6. Wellington, *South West Africa*, p. 154.
7. Vedder, *South West Africa in Early Times*, p. 260.

struggle was largely political; they feared that Jonker was growing so strong that he would soon completely dominate them.
The motives of the missionaries are more difficult to untangle.
The accounts of the missionaries themselves, as well as the
more historically minded missiological studies, quite naturally
stressed the theme that European Christians came to Africa as
the bearers of a superior civilization and as the prophets of
eternal salvation for the otherwise lost souls of heathendom. In
their reports and reminiscences, especially those destined to be
read by their supporters and financial backers in Europe, the
missionaries tended to portray Africa's native peoples as governed by "unspeakable abominations and vices" and themselves as a "handful of men, shut off from the rest of the
civilized world, so to speak, and struggling hopelessly, as it
were, [to persevere] in spite of disappointments." To prove
their noble calling, they stressed how much they were responsible for improving the conditions of native life, in that they
"made roads, kept up communication with the coast, built
houses, churches, schools, introduced agriculture . . . instructed
the natives in domestic science, needle and garden work, and
collected congregations at their several residences."[8]

This self-indulgent picture of selfless men working to bring
peace and order in a land where chaos and violence ruled was
only a part of the vision that missionaries held of their own
actions. They also clearly recognized that to convert the hea-
then and ennoble tribal lives with the blessings of civilization
they might be called upon to act vigorously as commercial
agents and political representatives of expanding European
colonial interests. If this involved them in the firearms trade, as
it frequently did, such participation could easily be rationalized
as an essential step in securing order on a "turbulent frontier"
by assisting those African leaders with whom they had established more or less amicable relations. Therefore, in 1870, the
German missionaries in South West Africa formed the Mis-
sions-Aktiengesellschaft with a capital of 708,000 marks; they
used this base to become, by the end of the 1880's, virtual

8. Wellington, *South West Africa*, pp. 160-161.

monopolists of the firearms trade to the colony. Similarly, when the missionaries appeared to act as agents of the German colonial administration by recruiting African labor for domestic or agricultural service, they argued that only by this means could they help bring peace to a troubled land and at the same time provide a suitable economic context within which to pursue the work of saving souls. While they may not have regarded their actions as contributing to the troubles they sought to allay, the actions they took are not wholly inconsistent from either a moral or a practical point of view. This point deserves special attention in view of the revisionist theme that has recently appeared in studies of the missionary role in Southern Africa. The revisionists, who come mainly from a group of East German historical scholars, have regarded the mission enterprise in German South West Africa as a sinister capitalist plot to cripple "the inner defensive strength of the land" and to create "favorable conditions for colonial conquest."[9]

Under the combined pressure of his allies and the missionaries, Jonker Afrikander signed the peace of Hoachanas in 1858 which brought an end to the Second Herero War. The treaty contained four major provisions: (1) the peace should embrace the whole country; (2) the Hereros should be included in the peace; (3) any one stealing cattle from the Hereros after the conclusion of the peace would be punished by a police force appointed for that purpose; (4) the police force should also be used to prevent the Hereros from encroaching on Nama territory.[10] The peace left Jonker the dominant figure in South West Africa. The Hereros feared him; the Namas, albeit with considerable reluctance, acknowledged him as their leader. At his camp at Windhoek, Jonker held several hundred Herero hostages as pledges for the good behavior of the tribe in the future. Then in 1861, three years after the peace was signed, Jonker died and with his death the power of the Orlams began to decline, for he alone had a reputation strong enough to forge a union of the Orlams and Namas. At about the same time a

9. See Loth, *Die Christliche Mission*, for a full exposition of this view.
10. The treaty is printed in full in Goldblatt, *History of South West Africa*, p. 27.

Swedish explorer-trader named Charles Andersson began selling guns in large numbers to the Hereros. For the first time
since the wars began, the two sides were more or less equally
armed. In 1863 the Hereros, using their new guns, rose against
the Namas. The "Herero War of Freedom," as this third war
was dubbed, lasted from 1863 to 1870. Though the Hereros were
successful in the opening campaigns, this war, like the previous
two, soon disintegrated into a formless contest consisting primarily of cattle raids. Nevertheless, when peace was made at
Okahandja in 1870 the Hereros were without doubt the winners,
in the sense that they were no longer in a subordinate position
to the Namas. More important for the future history of South
West Africa was the fact that white men had taken a direct part
in the struggle: on several occasions white officers had led the
Hereros into battle. More portentous was the fact that the white
residents of the land had petitioned both the Cape government
and the North German Federation for assistance in bringing
the tribal wars to an end. Though neither government respond-
ed, a dangerous precedent had been set.[11]

    The Peace of Okahandja lasted for a decade (1870-1880), a
remarkable record when one considers that in the preceding
forty years there had been only a bare ten years of peace. During
the peace the Herero chief, Maharero, emerged as the dominant
personality in South West Africa.[12] All the peoples—Namas,
Orlams, Hereros, and whites alike—looked to him to settle
their disputes, dispense justice, and keep the peace. Maharero
was flattered by his new-found power, but he was also very
much aware of the dangers inherent in the position he held.
Every decision he made alienated some group, left someone
dissatisfied. Realizing this, Maharero asked the Cape government to send a commissioner to South West Africa charged
with the task of keeping the peace. When an Orlam chief
warned Maharero that the Cape government was "digging a pit
for him," he answered: "That may well be, but I know you and
the Namas. I know, too, that you are my enemies. You stay

11. Vedder, *South West Africa in Early Times*, pp. 379-381.
12. *Ibid.*, 405-415.

where you are and leave me alone. If I have got to fall into a pit, I would rather fall into the Government's pit than into the hands of people like you who have been my enemies from the earliest days."[13] After protracted negotiations the Cape Government finally appointed one W. Coates Palgrave as Special Commissioner to South West Africa.[14] Maharero already knew Palgrave well and trusted him completely, but for that very reason the Namas were not at all inclined to submit to his authority. During his four years as Special Commissioner (1876-1880) Palgrave worked hard to create the basis for a lasting peace; but he was never able to win the confidence of the Namas, and since the Cape Government did not support his activities, he was in a hopeless position from the start. In 1880 a minor border incident triggered a renewal of tribal war and Palgrave withdrew, his mission a complete failure. With his withdrawal the last shred of European control disappeared, save for the British enclave at Walvis Bay. The missionaries and traders had no protection at all, and many of them were forced to leave their stations. The final tribal war lasted off and on for twelve years (1880-1892). As opposed to the previous wars, which stimulated trade, this one ruined the white traders. The exports from South West Africa to the Cape dropped from 138,886 marks in 1880 to 52,032 marks two years later. Most of the trading companies, including the Missionshandelsgesellschaft, went into receivership as a result of the war. When a representative of the Rhenish Missionary Society managed to patch together a temporary truce in 1882, the chain of events that would bring the presence of Imperial Germany to South West Africa was already underway.

The Coming of the Germans

The arrival of the Germans drastically changed the power relations in South West Africa. For two generations the Hereros

13. Wellington, *South West Africa*, p. 165.
14. Palgrave was a trouble-shooter for the Cape government. He joined the Cape police in 1869 and a few months later was sent to Kimberley as a magistrate. His mission to South West Africa in 1876 resulted in the annexation of Walvis Bay. At that time he had recommended the annexation of the whole of the territory.

had fought the Namas and their Orlam allies. We have no way of estimating the losses in the four wars, but they were without doubt heavy, particularly in the later struggles when all the participants had guns and plenty of ammunition. The wars served as a justification for German imperialism in South West Africa. Germans argued that one or the other of the contending tribes would eventually have eliminated the other and in this way ended the cycle of wars. The classic nineteenth-century justification for imperial expansion was that only by the imposition of *force majeure* could peace be brought to the uncivilized world, and without peace civilization was impossible.[15] The German colonial apologists used this argument effectively in the case of South West Africa, where it appeared to have a certain plausibility.

In the early 1880's German influence in South West Africa was stronger than that of any other European power, but for all that it was still miniscule. A few dozen traders, a handful of missionaries, and a prospector or two in a land half again as large as Germany constituted the whole of the German influence. Furthermore, the government in Berlin had shown no interest in imperial expansion. Bismarck had repeatedly emphasized that he had no interest in colonies. Under these circumstances the odds against the Germans establishing a colony in South West Africa seemed remote even on the eve of the event.

Sometime between 1880 and 1883, however, Bismarck reversed his position on the question of acquiring overseas possessions. Various explanations have been offered for his change of heart. Some historians have seen it as a part of a complicated diplomatic game in which the colonies were mere pawns. Others have tried to show that German traders and manufacturers got the ear of the chancellor and convinced him to change his mind. Still others have interpreted the whole colonial episode as some sort of accident—unplanned, unanticipated, and unwanted. Whatever the reason, by 1882 Bismarck was very much

15. This was the view expounded by the earliest missionaries, and it continued to dominate German colonial policy to the very end of the empire.

in a mood to listen to the proposals of a trader named Adolf Lüderitz, who asked him for a guarantee of imperial protection for such lands as he might acquire in Africa. Bismarck promised protection, but he made two conditions. First, Lüderitz must acquire a harbor, and second, any territories that he obtained must have a "clear title," by which he meant that no other power should have a competing claim to them.

With the tacit backing of Bismarck, Lüderitz sailed for Africa in early 1883. In May of that year he purchased the harbor of Angra Pequena (later renamed Lüderitz Bay), and twenty-five square miles surrounding it, from the Orlam chief Joseph Fredericks of Bethanie. The purchase price was 2500 marks, 200 rifles, and an assortment of toys including a number of lead soldiers. In August Lüderitz extended his holding by the purchase of a strip of coast 50 miles long and 20 miles wide to the north of Angra Pequena. Calling the combined purchases Lüderitzland, Lüderitz asked Bismarck to extend the promised imperial protection.

The chancellor, however, hesitated; he was not yet convinced that Lüderitz had indeed met his conditions. True, he had acquired a harbor, but the question remained whether the coast of South West Africa was within the British sphere of influence or not. Accordingly, the German government made a number of discreet inquiries to Whitehall "whether Her Majesty's Government exercised any authority in that locality. If so, the German Government would be glad if they would extend British protection to the German factory. If not, they [the German Government] will do their best to extend it the same measure of protection which they give to other subjects in remote parts of the world, but without having the least design to establish any footing in South Africa."[16] For several months the British government gave confusing and often contradictory answers. On some occasions the British professed to have no interest in the area at all; at other times they showed a marked disinclination to see any other power established north of the Orange; most

16. For a full discussion, see William Osgood Aydelotte, *Bismarck and British Colonial Policy* (Philadelphia, 1937). Also A. J. P. Taylor, *Germany's First Bid for Colonies* (Oxford, 1938).

often they claimed that the whole matter should properly be referred to the Cape Government. Bismarck finally wearied of this runaround and on April 24, 1884, he telegraphed the German consul in Capetown the following message: "According to statements of Mr. Lüderitz, the [British] Colonial Authorities do not believe that his acquisitions north of the Orange River should be entitled to German protection. You will declare officially that he and his establishments are under the protection of the Reich."[17]

During the next two years agents of Lüderitz as well as those of the German government expanded the initial holding so that by 1886 the whole of South West Africa was in some way in the German sphere of influence. Though Bismarck had not the slightest desire to exercise direct control over South West Africa, he did wish to create stable conditions there in which German traders and German missionaries could carry on their work. In order to bring about peace and order, Bismarck dispatched his Imperial Consul General and Commissioner for West Africa, Dr. Nachtigal, to the South West with orders to conclude treaties with the tribes of the interior. Nachtigal and his agents concluded protection treaties with Josef Fredericks of Bethanie, Piet Haibib, the captain of the Topnaars, and Hermanus van Wyk, the captain of the Reheboth Basters. Attempts to get other chiefs—in particular Kamaherero, the paramount chief of the Hereros, and Hendrik Witbooi—to accept German protection were in the first months unsuccessful.

In April 1885 Bismarck sent out Dr. Goering, the father of the Reichsfeldmarschall, as Imperial Commissioner for South West Africa with the task of completing the work of treaty-making. When Goering was actually in the process of negotiating with Kamaherero at his camp near Okahandja, Hendrik Witbooi arrived. At first the two chiefs, who were at the time nominally at peace, held a friendly parley, but presently a gun fight broke out. Goering not only watched the fight but even helped care for the Herero wounded. Though Kamaherero emerged from the affair victorious, the prospect of renewed war with the Witboois suddenly made German protection seem much more

17. Goldblatt, *History of South West Africa*, p. 88.

valuable than it had before. Therefore, on October 21, 1885, Kamaherero signed a protection treaty with Goering. With the signing of that treaty Hendrik Witbooi was the only major chief who still remained independent of Germany.

At first the Hereros were the mainstay of the German authority in South West Africa, but in 1888 Kamaherero had begun to question the value of the "protection" he was supposedly receiving from the Germans. So far as he was concerned, the treaty he had signed in 1885 was utterly useless because it gave him neither men, money, nor equipment with which to fight the Orlams. Finally, on October 30, 1888, Goering had to face the angry Hereros' leader at Okahandja. There Kamaherero told him that he repudiated the protection treaty as well as the agreements he had signed giving mineral rights to German companies. To add insult to injury, Kamaherero stated that he was giving an English adventurer named Robert Lewis power of attorney to exercise control and authority over the territory. As a result of this meeting the *Cape Times* reported that "the German protectorate at the South Western side of Africa is proving a melancholy farce." At the same time the Deutsche Kolonialgesellschaft für Südwestafrika had to inform the German government that it was near bankruptcy and would not be able to maintain any police or military forces in the colony. In view of the financial crisis the director of the company asked Bismarck to take over the protective measures. Bismarck answered that "it was not part of the Reich's functions and not in accordance with colonial policy, to restore State institutions among uncivilized peoples, and by means of military might to break down the opposition of Native chiefs to enterprises of German nationals which had not yet established themselves."[18] The missionaries, too, pleaded with Bismarck to send 400 men to bolster German authority, lest England or the Cape step in "or Lewis would render the stay of Germans intolerable." Despite all Bismarck's misgivings, the threat of English intervention tipped the balance, and on June 25, 1889, he sent 21 men commanded by Captain Curt von François to the colony to reassert German authority.

18. *Ibid.*, p. 109.

With the arrival of von François the German commitment in South West Africa assumed new dimensions. For better or for worse, South West Africa became a *German* colony and the direct responsibility of the German government. After the arrival of von François, German authority was dependent on military force and not on treaties. The people of South West Africa were to obey the Germans not because they had agreed to, but because the Germans had the force to coerce them. Von François's first act was to establish his headquarters at Windhoek, partly because it was strategically located in the center of the colony and unoccupied since the death of Jan Jonker, and partly because the lands around the town were the most promising for white settlement. No sooner had he arrived in Windhoek than he ordered the construction of a fort as an outward sign of German power. Von François also requested and received funds for the improvement of the harbor at Swakopmund so that he could be independent of the British harbor at Walvis Bay. In 1892 the first German colonists arrived and were settled in the vicinity of Windhoek. Within three years after the unceremonious dismissal of Goering the Germans had brought in all the trappings of modern colonialism: colonists, forts, armies, and officials. The commitment to stay had been made, not so much as a matter of government policy but by the decisions of the men on the spot. Speaking in the Reichstag on March 1, 1893, the German chancellor von Caprivi expressed his government's policy toward their colony in the following terms: "We have South West Africa. . . . I shall avoid retrospective consideration as to how we got it and whether it was a good thing or not—we have it. Now it is a German land and must remain a German land."[19] The key word is "must"; von Caprivi saw German policy in South West Africa as determined by a moral imperative.

The native peoples in South West Africa looked upon these signs of growing German domination with increasing apprehension. The leader of the party opposed to the Germans was Hendrik Witbooi, without a doubt the most impressive per-

19. Caprivi was so little interested in South West Africa that he once proposed selling it to the highest bidder.

sonality ever produced by the tribes of South West Africa. Hendrik was born in 1838, and in 1863, at the age of 25, was converted to Christianity; he soon learned to read high Dutch in a school run by the Rhenish mission. The Old Testament had a powerful influence on Hendrik, and more and more he saw himself cast in the role of leader of a Hebrew tribe doing battle with Amorites or Amalekites. He considered himself an instrument of the Lord to punish opposing tribes for their sins. In 1880 while in Hereroland, Hendrik was attacked by a group of Hereros. All his companions were killed but he survived—miraculously, it seemed—and on the way back to Namaland he had a vision: he saw all the Nama tribes united under a single leader doing battle against the Hereros.

In May of 1884 Hendrik split from his father. He explained this in the following fashion: "I have put my hand to the plough and I cannot turn back. I now request you to open the doors to the people who want to go with me, so that they may go, and to give them all horses and ammunition to help them on their way. You have no cause for anxiety. I am your son and I am going to act fairly toward you." He was now determined to lead his people into the promised land, which he identified as the rich pastures of the Hereros. When a missionary reproached him for his failure to honor his father, Hendrik countered by citing Samuel's acceptance of David as the leader of the Hebrews while Saul was still king. Most of the young Witboois flocked to Hendrik's banner. His first foray into Hereroland was a success, and a treaty was signed which gave Gobabis back to the Namas and also guaranteed Hendrik the right to go peacefully beyond the land of the Hereros to seek a place to settle. When the Rhenish missionaries closed down their missionary activities in Namaland, Hendrik, undismayed, proclaimed himself "summus episcopus in the native church." The *Deutsche Kolonialzeitung* reported that the Hottentots "believe in his mission and his vision and follow him." Before going north again, however, Hendrik first proceeded to subject all the Nama tribes to his authority.

In November 1892 Hendrik Witbooi and Samuel Maharero signed a peace treaty which not only ended the Fourth Herero

War (1880-1892) but also marked the first time that the natives of the land recognized that the greatest danger to their lives and possessions came not from one another but from the Germans. In a letter to the English magistrate at Walvis Bay, Hendrik Witbooi complained bitterly that the natives had signed treaties with the Germans in order to gain protection against their oppressors only to discover that the real oppressors were the Germans:

> The German himself is that person of whom he spoke, he is just what he described the other nations as . . . he makes no requests according to truth and justice and asks no permission of a chief. He introduces laws into the land . . . [which] are entirely impossible, untenable, unbelievable, unbearable, unmerciful and unfeeling. . . . He personally punishes our people at Windhoek and has already beaten people to death for debt. . . . It is not just and right to beat people to death for that. . . . He flogs people in a shameful and cruel manner. We stupid and unintelligent people, for so he thinks us to be, we have never yet punished a human being in such a cruel and improper way for he stretches people on their backs and flogs them on the stomach and even between the legs, be they male or female, so Your Honour can understand that no one can survive such a punishment.[20]

Hendrik Witbooi's alarm was well founded, for von François had come to the conclusion that the conquest of the Witboois was a necessary step in establishing effective German control over the land. To implement this policy he asked for and received 250 additional men from Germany. With these troops von François surrounded the Witbooi camp at Hornkranz and without any warning attacked it. The order issued by von François leaves no doubt about the objective of the attack: "The troops have the task of annihilating the Witbooi tribe," it read.[21] Although 150 Witboois were killed at Hornkranz (including 78 women and children), the attack was hardly a success from the German point of view. Not only did Hendrik manage to escape and rally the survivors, but he soon turned the tables on von François. In a daring raid Hendrik captured

20. Wellington, *South West Africa*, p. 179.
21. Horst Drechsler, *Südwestafrika unter Deutscher Kolonialherrschaft* (Berlin, 1966), p. 79.

most of the German horses, and without horses the German troops were immobilized. With the Germans stuck at Windhoek, Hendrik was free to roam at will over the southern half of the colony collecting men and equipment as he went. Six months after the "Massacre at Hornkranz" Hendrik's force numbered 600 men, double what it had been in the days following the German attack. And in addition, Hendrik had tripled his supply of horses and quadrupled his store of arms. In his most audacious act, he overran the German agricultural experiment station at Kubub and carried off 2350 merino sheep, 128 oxen, and 28 horses.

In Germany the reports from South West Africa at first caused anxiety and then anger. In the Reichstag the Socialist leader Bebel demanded an explanation for the murder of women and children at Hornkranz. When the government officials argued that the noncombatants had been killed because they had been used as shields, even the conservatives were left unsatisfied with the explanation. The *Vossische Zeitung* in an editorial stated bluntly that if von François was not able to end the war he should be replaced at once. Quite clearly von François's usefulness was at an end; but rather than replace him outright, the colonial officials decided to send an officer to examine the situation on the spot and make recommendations. The man selected was Major Theodor Leutwein, a professional officer with a classical education and a background in the law. He had no experience in colonial matters and knew nothing of Africa, but he had a reputation for being level-headed and judicious. In January 1894 Leutwein arrived at Windhoek. His superiors had told him that German power "must be maintained under all circumstances" and he was charged with the task of recommending how this end could be accomplished. In his memoirs Leutwein gave the following account of conditions as he saw them upon his arrival.

> The position in the territory on my arrival was certainly not rosy. . . . The natives stood against us as open enemies or at best in doubtful neutrality. Only the Basters of Rehoboth—just as today—were openly on our side. . . . Quite too long had the Empire delayed in showing its power to the natives. . . . Despite

our lack of power we had promulgated ordinances which the natives treated with contempt. Only the ordinances concerning arms and ammunition could be enforced because they were largely imported from the sea. Further we issued and ratified concessions over rights and territories that did not belong to us. In 1892, for example, we established a syndicate for land settlement to settle land stretching from Windhoek in the direction of Hoachanas and Gobabis. Yet at that time the robber Kharas-Hottentots occupied Gobabis. Hoachanas, after the expulsion of the Red Nation, was claimed by Captain Witbooi and these, as well as the Khauas-Hottentots, claimed that the boundaries of their authority lay close to the town of Windhoek. All this gave rise to the impression in the homeland that we were masters in the Protectorate. Actually up to 1894 the government had no power at all outside the capital, Windhoek. Even with the 1893 reinforcements the colonial troops were not strong enough to maintain government authority in the rest of the protectorate in addition to carrying on the war against the Witbooi.[22]

Leutwein's obvious grasp of the situation so impressed the colonial office in Berlin that in the late spring of 1894 he was made governor and military commander. Leutwein set to work immediately to restore German authority in the colony. His policy was dominated by two radically divergent ideas.[23] On the one hand he was determined to create in South West Africa a model European territorial state which, in effect, would become an extension of the German state, inhabited by Germans and governed by German laws. On the other hand, realizing that such a policy would result in the destruction of the existing tribal society and reduce the native population to the level of serfdom, Leutwein was determined to cushion the blow in every way that he could, so that the economic and psychological damage to the natives would be minimized.

In less than a year Leutwein had stabilized the German position in South West Africa. His strategy—and he was a master at it—was *divide et impera*. From the beginning he could count on the passive support of the Hereros, for they still

22. Theodor Leutwein, *Elf Jahre Gouverneur in Deutsch-Südwestafrika* (Berlin, 1906), p. 17.
23. The best discussion is in Helmut Bley, *Kolonialherrschaft und Sozialstruktur in Deutsch-Südwestafrika 1894-1914* (Hamburg, 1968).

believed that my enemy's enemy is my friend, and to them
Hendrik Witbooi was still *the* enemy. Leutwein shared their
point of view, but during his first months as governor he felt
that he was too weak to attack Hendrik directly. Instead, Leutwein spent the time overawing a number of minor Nama and
Orlam tribes and forcing them to accept German suzerainty. By
August 1894 three tribes, the people of Simon Kopper, the
Franzmannschen Hottentots, and the Khauas had bowed to
German power and acknowledged German "Oberherrschaft."
In a striking show of strength, Leutwein ordered the execution
of the Khauas chief for theft and murder. The other chiefs were
powerfully impressed both by the firmness of Leutwein and the
failure of the Khauas people to challenge the German decision.
At the same time that these minor tribes were being brought
into line Leutwein began the construction of a number of forts,
each stocked with an ample supply of ammunition and provisions and manned by a small garrison. These forts became the
overt symbols of the ever-expanding German power, daily re-
minders to the people that they were no longer free. By August
1894 Leutwein had effectively isolated Hendrik Witbooi. Leutwein called upon Hendrik to surrender, pointing out that compared to the German Kaiser, Hendrik was an insignificant
figure and for that reason would not suffer any shame or
humiliation in surrendering to him. Hendrik refused to bow to
German power. Thus rebuffed and confident that a military
victory was possible, Leutwein struck and struck hard. In just
over two weeks German repeating rifles and artillery convinced
Hendrik that war with the Germans was an unprofitable affair,
especially as Leutwein held out to him the bait of very lenient
terms. On September 15, 1894, Hendrik Witbooi signed a peace
treaty. In return for a promise to assist the Germans in any
future wars, the Witboois were allowed to retain their guns,
their horses, and their lands. As a check on the good behavior of
his new "allies," Leutwein sent a resident named von Burgsdorff to keep an eye on Hendrik Witbooi.
    After pacifying the colony Leutwein turned his attention to
the problem of encouraging European settlement, for he knew
that a lasting peace would only be assured when there was a

large permanent settlement of white colonists in South West Africa. The attempts of von François to settle German peasant farmers around Windhoek had been an economic failure. Profiting by this experience, Leutwein encouraged the whites to become cattle ranchers. As the best grazing land belonged to the Hereros, Leutwein reasoned that some of this land would have to be acquired before bringing settlers to South West Africa. To implement this policy Leutwein induced (bribed is probably a better word) Samuel Maharero to recognize a line running from Otjimbingwe in the west to Gobabis in the east as the southern boundary of Hereroland. As a corollary to this agreement, Samuel conceded that any cattle found south of the boundary were "ownerless" and could be sold by the German government. The proceeds from such sales were to be divided equally between Samuel and the Germans. For affixing his signature to this agreement Samuel was given a retainer of 2000 marks per year.

The legality of the document was open to question on several grounds, not the least of which was the fact that the land which Samuel so blithely sold was not his to sell: by Herero tribal custom, all land was held in common and the chief had no special rights over it beyond those of a member of the tribe. Even more blatant was the fact that Samuel had signed away a good portion of the land of the eastern Hereros, over whom he had no authority whatsoever. As soon as the cattle confiscations began, the eastern Hereros decided to resist. What was called "War of the Boundary" erupted in March 1896 and was ended by the Germans within a few weeks. Leutwein's divide-and-rule policy paid handsome dividends during the war. Not only did all the remaining tribes maintain a benevolent neutrality; some even gave assistance to the Germans. In particular, Hendrik Witbooi in accordance with his treaty obligations sent a large contingent of scouts. For their part in the uprising the eastern Herero chiefs Nikodemus and Kakimena were executed and their peoples disarmed.

With the conclusion of the "War of the Boundary" peaceful development of the colony proceeded apace, stimulated by the construction of the Swakopmund-Windhoek railroad. By the time the railroad was completed in 1903 the white population of the colony had risen to 4640, about two-thirds of whom were German. The majority of the settlers were cattle ranchers. The rise of the white cattlemen took place concurrently with the decline of the Herero herdsmen. That proud tribe suffered the torments of Job in the last years of the old century and the first years of the new. In 1897 the rinderpest struck, carrying off 80 to 90 percent of their cattle. Five years later the Herero herds were estimated to be only about 50,000, or half of what they had been before the epozootic hit. During this disaster the German herds, which received timely inoculations, fared much better than those of the Hereros. By 1902 some 1,051 whites owned almost as many cattle as 80,000 Hereros. After the rinderpest came a typhus epidemic which killed an estimated 10,000 Hereros. Even more important than these natural disasters were the man-made blows which threatened not only the economic basis of the tribe but also its cultural vitality. From 1896 to 1903 the Hereros saw much of their best land and a good portion of their cattle pass into the hands of the white man. Each year Hereros "sold" thousands of head of cattle to white traders. The system of selling was well described by a German officer who watched it in operation.

> The Herero brings the oxen which he wishes to sell. 'How much do you want for the oxen?' says the trader. 'Fifty pounds sterling,' replies the Herero. 'Good' says the trader, 'here you have a coat valued at £20, trousers worth £10 and coffee and tobacco worth £20, that is all £50.' The Herero is satisfied: he knows that according to the customs of the traders he cannot expect more for his cattle. He may probably exchange the coat for a blanket and get some sugar in lieu of the tobacco, and he will also (as is customary) by begging get a little extra; if, however, he does not succeed the transaction is closed. It will be admitted that this sort of trading is exceptional and quite original; it requires to be learned and the newcomer will have to pay for his experience, before he is able to emulate the dodges and tricks of the old traders.[24]

From the standpoint of the natives the worst aspect of this sort of "trading" was the practice of extending credit. The

24. Wellington, *South West Africa*, p. 191.

trader would give goods to Hereros if they would promise to make payment at some later date. When the time came to pay, the trader would demand interest, which in many cases was many times greater than the original debt. Though Leutwein tried to prevent the worst abuses of the credit system, he was not successful in the face of the strenuous objections of the local white population.

The loss of cattle, serious as it was, did not endanger the corporate existence of the tribe, but the alienation of land meant that Herero herdsmen would some day be replaced by white ranchers. Leutwein supported this policy, as did nearly every other white man in the colony with the exception of a few missionaries. As the colonial propagandist Paul Rohrbach explained the land problem, it all sounded very logical and necessary.

> The decision to colonize in South Africa means nothing less than that the Native tribes must withdraw from the lands on which they have pastured *their* cattle and so let the *White man* pasture *his* cattle on the selfsame lands. If the moral right of this standpoint is questioned, the answer is that for people of the cultural standard of South African Natives, the loss of their free national barbarism and the development of a class of workers in the service of and dependent on the Whites is primarily a law of existence in the highest degree. For a people, as for an individual, an existence appears to be justified in the degree that it is useful in the progress of general development. By no argument in the world can it be shown that the preservation of any degree of national independence, national prosperity, and political organization by the races of South West Africa would be of greater or even equal advantage for the development of mankind in general or the German people in particular than that these races should be made serviceable in the enjoyment of their former territories by the White Races.[25]

Rohrbach gave the rationale; greed was the driving force; weakness was the temptation. Year by year vast tracts of Herero land passed from tribal ownership into the hands of the white settlers. Samuel Maharero was the conduit for these transactions and the principal beneficiary. For pitifully small sums he was willing to alienate the tribal lands of his own people and of

25. *Ibid.*, p. 196.

other tribes as well. By 1903 more than 25 percent of all Herero land (3,500,000 hectares out of 12,000,000) had already passed out of native hands. At the rate of alienation that prevailed in 1903 it would have taken only a few more years for the Hereros to be completely dispossessed. Leutwein was alarmed at this prospect, as were many of the missionaries. Consequently in 1903 serious discussions were initiated with the object of working out a plan for setting up a native reserve which would guarantee some lands to the Hereros in perpetuity. Samuel Maharero, it should be noted, feared that the lands would be too large and thereby limit his profits from land sales; the missionaries and most of the Herero people, on the other hand, feared that the reserve would be too small to permit the continued existence of the tribe.

By the end of 1903 the situation in Hereroland had reached a crisis. Weakly led, demoralized, and impoverished, the Hereros were growing desperate. The seeds of a revolt, sown many years beforehand, had long germinated and now only needed an incident to bring them forth.

Colonial Administration

Bismarck had wanted a colonial empire at limited cost. "The German Empire cannot carry on a system of colonization like that of France," he once declared. "It cannot send out warships to conquer territory overseas, that is, it will not take the initiative; but [it] will protect the German merchant even in the land which he acquires. Germany will do what England has always done, establish Chartered Companies; so that the responsibility always rests with them."[26] On another occasion the Iron Chancellor explained: "I would follow the example of England in granting to these merchants something like Royal Charters. . . . I do not wish to found provinces, but to protect commercial establishments in their own development. . . . We hope that the tree will flourish in proportion to the activity of the gardener, but if it does not, the whole responsibility rests with him and

---

26. Mary Townsend, *The Rise and Fall of Germany's Colonial Empire 1884-1918* (New York, 1930), p. 119.

not with the empire, which will lose nothing."[27] In line with this policy Bismarck did no more than extend "protection" to Lüderitzland in 1884. Lüderitz himself imported botanists, geographers, mining engineers, and other experts to map out his new possessions and determine their economic potential. Their reports were uniformly discouraging. Finding that his lands contained little or nothing of value, Lüderitz began negotiations with an English company to sell his holdings.

To Bismarck, this would not do. The German government had expended too much diplomatic capital in acquiring the protectorate to let it go to a handful of English traders. It turned out that South West Africa had to be maintained to prevent Germany from looking foolish in the eyes of the world. Therefore, prodded by Bismarck, a group of prominent German businessmen, including the bankers Bleichröder and von Hansemann, formed the Deutsche Südwestafrika Gesellschaft and bought out Lüderitz for half a million marks. Having acquired his holdings the company sent out three expeditions to survey their new possession. The reports of these expeditions were as discouraging as those of Lüderitz. There was no evidence of mineral wealth; stock-raising was impossible except on the central plateau, which was not controlled by the company; and the best guano beds were in English hands. At the end of one year of operation the Deutsche Südwestafrika Gesellschaft reported a total loss of 45,159 marks and no prospects of improving the balance sheet. Under these circumstances the board of directors was unwilling to accept Bismarck's offer of a charter, which would have saddled them with the expense and responsibility of ruling the area. As the company would not accept the task of ruling the coastal regions and was too weak to rule the interior, Bismarck, against his better judgment, dispatched an Imperial commissioner, Dr. Heinrich Goering, to administer the former Lüderitzland as well as Hereroland and Namaland. In 1888, as has been related, the Hereros unceremoniously threw him out. Bismarck then saw no alternative but to do what he had sworn he would never do, namely send colonial troops to impose German rule on the area. In 1889 he defended his

27. *Ibid.*

policy in the Reichstag. "I repeat that I am opposed to colonies, that is, the kind of colonies where officials must be placed and garrisons established. . . . My present action is dictated only by pressing necessity. . . . I cannot burden myself with the reproaches of posterity that I failed to protect Germans and German territory. . . . If the locomotive of the empire has struck out on a new track for itself, I will not be the one to put stones in its way. . . . Von Haus aus bin ich kein Kolonialmensch and I entertain the gravest apprehension on the subject, but I submit to the pressure of public opinion, I yield to the majority."[28]

When Bismarck authorized the sending of von François and 20 men to South West Africa, he committed the German nation to the task of imposing their rule by force on the area. After Bismarck's dismissal in 1890, the new chancellor, von Caprivi, formalized his predecessor's commitment to colonialism by setting up a section in the Foreign Office (the Kolonialabteilung) whose sole function was the administration of the colonial empire. Following the dictates of Parkinson's Law, the new section grew rapidly. Before long the Kolonialabteilung was giving advice to travelers, publishing a news letter (the *Kolonialblatt*), preparing memoranda for ministers, and doing the preliminary work on the budget. To meet the complaint that the Kolonialabteilung was staffed with bureaucrats who knew nothing at all about the colonies, von Caprivi set up an advisory board, the Kolonialrat, on which sat 20 (later 40) experts who had experience in the colonies or economic interest in them. More important in shaping German policy vis-à-vis the colonies than either the Kolonialabteilung or the Kolonialrat was an unofficial organization called the Deutsche Kolonialgesellschaft (DK). At the time of the Herero uprising, the DK had about 35,000 members. The president was always a well-known German citizen with good connections in both the political and the economic worlds. The DK sponsored various educational activities and published a number of periodicals, including the *Zeitschrift für Kolonialpolitik und Kolonialwirtschaft* and the *Tropenpflanzer*. The members of the society

28. *Ibid.*, p. 157.

included virtually all influential Germans who believed that Germany's destiny was somehow or other bound up with the colonial empire. During the long war in South West Africa, when many Germans grew discouraged with the whole idea of colonialism, it was the DK that kept the pressure on the Reichstag and the government.

3

The Initial Blow

IN THE AUTUMN of 1903 the German administrators and officials in South West Africa were quietly confident that the colony was advancing in an orderly way along the path that led to "civilization."[1] Since the last uprising in 1896, law and order had, for the most part, prevailed. Year after year Leutwein had traveled throughout the colony visiting the chiefs and dispensing justice. In the summer of 1903 he had demanded that the old chief Tjetjo and his tribe turn in all their weapons. Backed by the support of Samuel Maharero, who had been a long-time enemy of Tjetjo, Leutwein was able to enforce compliance without recourse to arms.[2] The whole incident seemed to prove that the Hereros had lost the will to resist the white man. Leutwein was so convinced that the blacks had lost all stomach for fighting that in the autumn of 1903 he withdrew over half of the troops stationed in Hereroland for duty in the extreme south of the colony.

Yet beneath the tranquil surface there was growing bitterness among the Hereros, and indeed most of the other tribes as well, at the treatment they received at the hands of the German settlers and traders. On the eve of the rebellion a Herero told a German officer that "if the Herero is angry and storms at you there is nothing to fear, but when he laughs and is friendly be on your guard. . . . Sir, they are so crafty that [even] if you

1. Bley, *Kolonialherrschaft*, pp. 160ff., for a detailed analysis.
2. Kurt Schwabe, *Mit Schwert und Pflug in Deutsch-Südwestafrika* (Berlin, 1904), p. 67.

understand their speech and sit with them at the fire, they can be deciding your death whilst you think they are talking about flowers."[3] And so it was in the last days of 1903; the Germans deluded themselves into thinking their subject peoples were quiescent when in reality they were planning an uprising that would shake the German rule to its foundation.

The Causes of the Uprising

By 1904 the Hereros had so many reasons for rebelling that it might be more profitable to ask why they had not acted sooner, rather than why they revolted when they did. First, every Herero was alarmed at the progressive loss of land. Up to 1900 only a minor portion of the Herero hereditary lands had been alienated, but with the completion of the railroad to Windhoek the pace of alienation accelerated rapidly, so that by the end of 1903 three and one-half million hectares out of a total of thirteen million had been lost, and the day when the Hereros would not have enough land to continue their traditional way of life was fast approaching. In 1903 the German colonial economist, Paul Rohrbach, was made Siedlungskommissar and given a budget of 300,000 marks to encourage German settlement. Although his views were perfectly straightforward, the German attitude alarmed the Africans, and their alarm was compounded when they learned that Leutwein was considering a plan to create tribal reserves, or reservations. In the abstract, of course, reserves had many advantages, but the Hereros feared that the whites would take all the good land and they would be left with the Omaheke desert.

When District Chief Zürn in Okahandja called the Herero leaders together in late 1903 in order to gain their assent for a reserve plan, the leaders objected on three grounds: first, the area was too small; second, it was too arid; third, it was too remote. The meeting broke up with Zürn testily announcing that he did not need approval.[4] Leutwein's motives are subject to various in-

3. Wellington, South West Africa, p. 203.
4. Drechsler, Südwestafrika, p. 145.

terpretations. He himself said that he wanted to curb the incursions of rapacious land dealers before they gained possession of all the valuable land in South West Africa. To many Hereros, however, the reserves looked very much like a scheme to force them into such a small area that they would be forced to give up their traditional way of life and work for the white man in order to survive. However one interprets the reserve scheme, it had the effect of alarming the Hereros, particularly the younger men who were rapidly growing disillusioned with the appeasement policy of the tribal elders.

Even more important than the German threat to create reservations was the beginning of the construction of the Otavi railroad. As in the case of the Swakopmund-Windhoek line, the construction company was given title to a wide strip of land on either side of the railroad, but whereas the Swakopmund-Windhoek line ran along the southern boundary of Hereroland, the Otavi line ran straight through the heart of it. The company was to receive not only blocks of land twenty by ten kilometers but also all the water rights. Leutwein was confident that he could persuade Samuel Maharero to agree to this massive amputation of Herero land, but only if it was in some way disguised. As he wrote at the time: "A land transfer of the magnitude desired by the company simply cannot be carried out at this time. The chiefs have requested that the native villages in the path of the railroad not be forced to relocate, but only move as much as is actually necessary. Yet it is to be anticipated after the experience we had with the building of the government railroad, the natives, who do not really like to be located near a major transportation system will, in due time, leave of their own accord if they find sufficient water elsewhere."[5] Bebel, the leader of the Social Democratic party in the Reichstag, spoke of the Otavi line in this vein: "The Hereros have already been robbed of a large part of their land and have had to move further east. But if they now hear that the new railroad construction is planned which, according to their experience thus far, will result in further loss of their land and thereby threaten their existence, who can blame them if they do everything in

5. *Ibid.*, p. 151.

their power to defend their property?" Even Samuel Maherero, who up to 1903 had a long record of cooperation with the Germans in the systematic alienation of his people's land, was not willing to support the Germans on this question.

The gradual loss of land, frightening as it was to any Herero who looked only a few years into the future, did not yet, in 1903, affect the daily life of the Hereros. The problem of debt was another matter. For many years Hereros had fallen into the habit of borrowing money from white traders at usurious rates of interest.[6] Leutwein had long been concerned about this practice, which he considered immoral and politically explosive, but all his attempts to find a solution had been frustrated by the powerful colonial interests which grew rich on the profits. Finally, on July 23, 1903, Leutwein grasped the nettle and issued an ordinance which provided that all outstanding debts which were not collected within a year would be null and void.[7] The ordinance went into effect on November 1, 1903. This law, whose sole purpose was to wipe the slate clean after a reasonable period of time and then discourage further abuses of the credit system, had—in the short run—the opposite effect. The German traders, knowing that if they did not collect all outstanding debts within a year they would lose them forever, not unnaturally began recalling their loans as quickly as possible. To facilitate the collection process government officials, and on some occasions even soldiers, were pressed into service to aid the traders. In some cases traders turned over lists of their debtors to local officials; in others, the traders themselves expropriated as many cattle as they thought necessary to cover claims—and, as one trader remarked, a few extra to cover any future claims.[8] The resentment of the Hereros toward the trad-

6. Wellington, *South West Africa*, pp. 190-191.

7. Leutwein, *Elf Jahre*, p. 559. Leutwein said that the government had not issued the ordinance out of any love for the natives but rather to preserve the life and possessions of those whites who were then living among the natives.

8. See Wellington, *South West Africa*, pp. 198-199, and Drechsler, *Südwestafrika*, pp. 147-149. The Hereros named each year according to the most significant event which occurred during its course. The year 1902 was named "ojovuronde juviuego," which meant the year of traders and fraud.

ers was understandably great, and it was compounded by a feeling of hopelessness when the German officials were seen to be aiding and abetting the traders. Moderate German newspapers were almost unanimous in citing the credit ordinance as the principal reason for the uprising. On January 25, 1904, the *Kölnische Zeitung* editorialized: "The credit ordinance . . . is one of the direct causes of dissatisfaction among the Hereros. The dubious past of the traders in Europe is quite often the reason for their being down there in the first place."

In the opinion of present-day East German scholars, the naked economic exploitation of the natives was the sole reason for the rebellion, and they mock bourgeois historians who claim that the conflict grew out of irreconcilable racial and cultural differences. Yet the economic explanation is too simple. Racial tension was real and very intense by 1903. Every year saw more and more white settlers coming into the colony "as conquerors, in a land which had not yet been conquered," as Leutwein put it.[9] Typically these new settlers were ne'er-do-wells, and not a few of them were criminally inclined younger sons of the aristocracy, packed off to darkest Africa to prevent them from disgracing the family name at home. The old colonial hands like Leutwein had a real respect for Africans as men, because they knew them as soldiers and because they had fought against them. The newer arrivals saw the black Africans at best as nothing but a potential source of cheap labor, and some even raised the question whether the colony would not be better off if the black population were completely eliminated. Indeed, when the rebellion broke out, a number of settlers voiced the opinion that the uprising was a positive advantage since it gave the Germans a chance to annihilate the natives. The consciousness of being white, which had no doubt played a major role in German actions from the very beginning, became a dominant factor for those colonists who came with wives and children. In 1903 there were about 4000 white males in South West Africa and only 700 white women. The inevitable result of this imbalance was what the Germans referred to as "Verkafferung" or

9. For the most perceptive analysis of Leutwein's attitude, see Bley, *Kolonialherrschaft*.

"Schmutzwirtschaft." From the perspective of the natives, "Ver-kafferung" meant that the German men took their women, peacefully if possible, but otherwise by force. In 1903 a par-ticularly nasty, but by no means unusual, incident took place, and it went far toward convincing most Hereros that their very survival as men depended on driving the Germans out of their land. Leutwin's account of the affair is worth quoting in its entirety, not so much for what he includes as for what he leaves out:

> In the early part of 1903 an intoxicated white man shot a Herero woman, who was sleeping peacefully in a wagon. He did this be-cause he thought he was being attacked and so he fired blindly in all directions. The court rejected the contention that he was actually being attacked, so the case turned on the question of the hallucinations of a drunkard. The judges found the man not guilty because they accepted the defense that he had acted in good faith. This acquittal aroused extraordinary excitement in Hereroland, especially since the murdered woman was the daugh-ter of a chief. Everywhere the question was asked: "Have the white people the right to shoot native women?" I traveled to Hereoland to pacify the people as far as I was able and also to make clear to them that I did not agree with the judgment of the court, but that I had no influence over it. Luckily the prosecutor appealed. The accused was then brought before the Supreme Court in Windhoek and sentenced to three years imprisonment. The event, however, had contributed its share toward the unrest among the Hereros which resulted in the outbreak of the rebel-lion a half year later.[10]

Leutwein's account, while not actually mendacious, leaves out a good deal. The trader's name was Dietrich, and on the day the incident occurred he was going by foot to the town of Omaruru. While on the trail he was overtaken by a wagon driven by the son of a Herero chief. The young man was accompanied by his wife and child. Upon being offered a ride Dietrich climbed on the wagon. When night fell they made camp. In the middle of the night the young Herero heard screams and then a shot. Upon investigation he found his wife dead, shot by Dietrich, who had killed her when she resisted his

10. *Report on the Natives of South West Africa and Their Treat-ment by Germany* (London, 1918), p. 55.

attempts to rape her. In a confidential report sent to the Colonial Office in Berlin, Leutwein admitted that Dietrich's story about believing he was being attacked was a total fabrication.[11] It is worth noting that after the outbreak of the rebellion Dietrich was released and made a noncommissioned officer in the volunteer force.

In Leutwein's memoirs he frankly admits that for all practical purposes the white population had suffered nothing at the hands of the natives before January 1904, whereas the natives had been grievously abused. He concludes: "The fundamental causes of the outbreak are two-fold: the Hereros from early years were a freedom-loving people, conquering and proud beyond measure. On the one hand there was the progressive extension of the German rule over them and on the other their own sufferings under pressure from year to year. But, and this is decisive, they had the impression that in regard to this rule of the Germans they were in the last resort the stronger side."[12] His last point is disputed by most of the documentary evidence we possess, but Leutwein knew the Hereros well and his evidence cannot be rejected out of hand. It is not inconceivable that the older, more experienced leaders like Henrik Witbooi and Samuel Maharero were defeatists from the start, but that the younger men, who by all accounts pushed the leaders into action, misread the situation to the extent of believing that they could defeat the Germans and drive them out of South West Africa.

White settlers normally referred to black Africans as "baboons" and treated them accordingly. As one missionary reported: "The real cause of the bitterness among the Hereros toward the Germans is without question the fact that the average German looks down upon the natives as being about on the same level as the higher primates (baboon being their favorite term for the natives) and treats them like animals. The settler holds that the native has a right to exist only in so far as he is useful to the white man. It follows that the whites value their horses and even their oxen more than they value the natives."[13]

11. *Ibid.*, 54-55.
12. Quoted in Goldblatt, *History*, p. 138.
13. Drechsler, *Südwestafrika*, p. 349.

This contempt for the black African was held to be the reason for the many acts of violence that whites perpetrated on the Hereros. Indeed, settlers were wont to explain such behavior in quasi-medical terms, inventing a disease called "tropical frenzy" which was said to overtake white men in the tropics. A German doctor writing in 1902, however, rejected such an explanation: "I have never found anywhere any evidence of the disease which in the accounts of murders in the daily newspapers from the colonies plays such a role, that is, 'tropical frenzy.' . . . There are a relatively large number of men of a passionate temperament among the Europeans in the colonies because the average man of mild temperament would rather remain in his own homeland. For a man of weak character there are, out under the palms, opportunities greater than in Europe to avoid the moral imperatives."[14] Nor was this contemptuous attitude confined to settlers. The Kaiser and his Chief of Staff displayed attitudes hardly different from those of the average settler in South West Africa.[15] When Matthias Erzberger, speaking in the Reichstag, pointed out that the black men had immortal souls just as the Germans did, he was hooted down by the whole right side in the house.[16]

Such, then, was the temper of the whites and blacks in Hereroland on the eve of the rebellion. The Hereros, or at least a large portion of them, had decided that German rule meant not only personal humiliation and economic ruin but the end of their traditional way of life. Given this conviction they saw little reason to wait and see if conditions would improve. By 1903 the tinder was ready and only a spark was needed to set Hereroland aflame. That spark was provided in an unexpected way, and from an unexpected quarter. Almost 500 miles to the south of Windhoek lived a Hottentot tribe called the Bondelzwarts.[17] Their land, which lay between the Karras Hills and the

14 *Ibid.*

15. Bernhard, Prince von Bülow, *Memoirs* (4 vols., Berlin, 1931), I, p. 24. The Kaiser said, among other things, that Christian precepts were not applicable to heathens and savages.

16. Klaus Epstein, "Erzberger and the German Colonial Scandals, 1905-1910," *English Historical Review* (LXXIV, 1959), p. 637.

17. See Military Section, German General Staff, eds., *Die Kämpfe der deutschen Truppen in Südwestafrika* (2 vols., Berlin, 1907), I, 19-23, for a detailed account. Hereafter cited as *Official History*.

Orange river, was bleak and arid. Just how many Bondelzwarts there were was not known; the Germans, however, estimated that the tribe could muster somewhere between 300 and 700 warriors. A total of 161 white men lived in the area; included in this number was the military force, which consisted of one officer, three noncommissioned officers, twelve men, and two civilian policemen. Since 1890 the Bondelzwarts had lived in peace with the Germans because they considered Hendrik Witbooi to be their real enemy.

Then, in 1903, the local German authorities ordered the Bondelzwarts to register their guns. This demand, which the Bondelzwarts correctly interpreted as a prelude to total disarmament, was rejected by their chief, Willem Christian. To enforce compliance the district chief, a Lieutenant Jobst, accompanied by five men, rode into the encampment of Willem Christian. A fire-fight ensued in which three Germans were killed and a fourth wounded. Four days later (October 29, 1903) Leutwein in Windhoek received news of the affair. He at once dispatched the Third Field Company from Keetmanshoop and the First Field Company from Windhoek to restore order in the south. When after a month of desultory fighting the situation had not improved but had actually deteriorated, since the Bondelzwarts were by then cooperating with small bands of robbers who infested the Karras Hills, Leutwein himself went to the south to take personal command. So serious did he judge the situation that on December 25, 1903, he ordered Captain Franke and the Second Field Company to head south from their home base at Omaruru. With the departure of Franke, Hereroland was nearly emptied of German troops: only a company far to the north at Outjo and a battery at Okahandja were left to guard 25,000 square miles and 20 towns.

The Hereros sensed at once that they had an opportunity that might not come again. However, the absence of the soldiers and Leutwein was also a danger to them. No sooner was the restraining hand of Leutwein removed than the settlers began pushing the natives, hoping to drive them to some desperate act which would permit a final solution to the "black problem." The Hereros trusted Leutwein (whom they called "Majora," with a mixture of deference and affection), but to the whites he was a traitor to his race. "Leniency towards blacks is cruelty towards whites," as one colonial apologist put it.[18] After Leutwein departed, rumors were abroad in the land, most of them apparently inspired by the settlers. On the one hand, it was said that Leutwein and 75 men had been killed, or according to another version driven across the frontier and interned by the British. On the other hand, there were reports that the British had invaded South West Africa and were marching north to drive the Germans out. Samuel Maharero described the situation in Hereroland after the departure of Leutwein in the following way:

> And now in those days the white people said to us that you [Leutwein] who were at peace with us and loved us, were gone, and they said to us: The governor who loved you has gone to fight a difficult war; he is dead and because he is dead you [Hereros] must also die. They went so far as to kill two men of Chief Tjetjo's tribe. Even Lieutenant N began to kill my people in jail. Ten died and it was said they died of sickness, but they died at the hands of the labor overseer and by the lash.
>
> Eventually Lieutenant N began to treat me so badly and to look for a reason for killing me, so he said: the people of Kambasembi and Uanja are making war. Then he called me to question me, I answered truthfully 'No,' but he did not believe me. At last he hid soldiers in boxes in the fort and he sent for me, so when I came he could shoot me. I did not go; I saw his intentions and so I fled. . . . Because of these things I became angry and said 'Now I must kill the white people even if I die.'[19]

To be sure, Samuel was writing after the outbreak of the rebellion and was trying to justify his actions to Leutwein, but Leutwein, who quoted the letter, admitted that Samuel's account was substantially correct. Chief Zacharias gave a similar account of the outbreak. He said he knew that if he revolted his tribe would be annihilated but that "the cruelty and unjustices"

18. Paul Rohrbach, the colonial propagandist, is generally credited with this formulation, but the idea was commonplace among the settlers in South West Africa.

19. The letter, in a slightly modified version, is reproduced in Leutwein, *Elf Jahre*, p. 512.

of the Germans had driven his people to the point where death had lost its terrors.

The Opposing Forces

The total number of German soldiers on active duty in German South Africa in January 1904, after deductions have been made for men on leave and those on the sick list, were as follows:[20]

Line Officers	27
Medical Officers	9
Veterinarian Officers	3
Paymaster	1
Other ranks	726
Total	766

About two-thirds of these men were assigned to the field force; the remainder either had administrative duties or were serving in the capacity of local policemen. The field troops were divided into four companies of mounted infantry and one company of artillery. The infantry companies were stationed at Keetmanshoop, Omaruru, Outjo, and Windhoek and the artillery was at Okahandja. Each company was in turn divided into two sections: one was kept intact at the main base while the other was broken up and stationed at smaller posts within the district. In addition to the men on active duty there was a large trained reserve in the colony numbering 34 officers and 730 men. Most of these reservists had served in the colonial forces, and upon discharge they had been induced to stay in South West Africa in return for large grants of land. Beyond the reserves there was a pool of about 400 able-bodied men with no military training, though most of them were good horsemen and proficient with the rifle. Furthermore, the Germans had available to them 120 Baster scouts and a slightly larger number of Witboois to serve as auxiliaries.

Taken all together, the Germans had approximately 2000 men available for service. The German soldiers were armed with the Model 88 rifle, an excellent weapon which in the

20. *Official History*, II, 12ff (cited in note 17).

hands of a good shot could kill a man at ranges up to half a mile. Though German artillery was limited to five modern quick-firing mountain guns and five older pieces, even these ten guns were of great military significance, because the Hereros held any artillery in awe and tended to avoid contact with troops accompanied by field pieces. Finally, the Germans had five Maxim guns, the total firepower of which was probably not much less than that of all the native weapons put together.[21] As the English writer Belloc put it: "Whatever happens we have got/The Maxim gun and they have not." Since von François built the first fort at Windhoek in the early 1890's, several dozen more forts had been constructed. All were sturdily built with massive walls enclosing barracks, armory, storehouses, and other buildings. There was the inevitable watchtower rising above the walls, giving the defenders a clear and unobstructed view of the surrounding countryside. In all cases the forts were supplied with a secure source of water and in their storehouses was a plentiful supply of food and ammunition, so that in case of emergency the garrison could hold out for up to a year without outside assistance. The whole network of forts was bound together by a telegraph system and for emergencies a number of heliographs were available.

Opposed to this modern force were some 8000 Herero warriors. Just how many had weapons is a matter of some dispute. Leutwein estimated that not more than one-half of them were armed with rifles, but the editors of the German official history imply that the number might have been much larger than this. The editors point out that between 20,000 and 30,000 handguns of various types were imported into South West Africa in the generation before the outbreak of the rebellion. The Germans had, to be sure, confiscated some of these and many must have been worn out in normal service, but if these figures are correct then there must have been considerably more than 4000 guns in Hereroland. More critical than guns was ammunition, and

21. During the First World War, French military writers estimated that one well-placed machine gun amply supplied with ammunition had sufficient firepower to pin down a brigade of infantry (approximately 6000 men).

there all commentators agree the Hereros were generally in short supply. What impressed the Germans the most about the Hereros was their military sophistication and ability to learn from experience. Indeed, the editors of the German official history argue that the Hereros bore little resemblance to the native warriors of the European imagination, who "armed with spear and sword charged into the fire of their enemy and let themselves be mowed down by machine guns." Instead, the Hereros, because of their tribal discipline and warlike traditions, proved to be man for man equivalent to the German soldiers. "In battle it is immaterial whether the skin of the fighter is white or black," wrote the editors, "it is only a question of whether the fighter understands how to take cover in grass or brush or behind boulders and then get a steady bead. Our enemies compared favorably in terms of cleverness and marksmanship with the Boers. . . . In military value and determination they surpassed the Boers by a wide margin."[22]

The Initial Blow

During the last days of 1903 and the first of 1904 the Hereros made their final plans for a concerted attack which, they hoped, would undermine the sources of German power in their land. Their greatest single advantage was the element of surprise, and they exploited it to the utmost. Leutwein knew Samuel Maharero very well and was absolutely convinced that the old chief was far too fond of the good life, particularly of alcohol and women, to take up arms against his friends and patrons the Germans—who, after all, supplied him with the wherewithal to sustain his pleasures. Leutwein said of Samuel that he was "a large man, imposing and of proud mien, a man not without spirit and understanding"; but he added that Samuel was "lacking in character" and sacrificed the duties of his office of Paramount Chief to pleasure. Leutwein was convinced that without Samuel's name and authority no common action on the part of the Hereros was possible, but he confessed that he

22. *Official History*, I, 19.

had no evidence on which to decide whether Samuel was the initiator of the revolt or whether he was forced into it by others. At the time many Germans in the colony speculated that the real force behind the revolt was Assa-Riarua, the son of Samuel's half-brother Riarua, and a man who was known to have a passionate hatred of the Germans. Leutwein concluded his analysis of Samuel's reasons for leading the revolt with the observation that only two things could have forced Samuel to act: first, the fear of the loss of his own position, and second, the rumor that he (Leutwein) had been killed. Looking back on such shreds of evidence as we have, it seems highly probable that the plans for an uprising had been laid many months before. In April and May of 1903 the Herero headmen held a long series of meetings in Okahandja, and though they assured the German authorities that they were only discussing routine tribal matters, the weight of circumstantial evidence suggests that it was at these meetings that the initial plans were laid.

The ultimate objective of the revolt was, of course, to drive the Germans out of South West Africa or at least out of Hereroland. This goal was to be achieved by undermining the German power structure from two different angles. First, an attack was to be made on German outposts and garrisons as well as on the transportation and communication system, with the objective of crippling German military power so that the German government would lose the ability to protect the colony. Second, an all-out attack was to be made on the German farmers. They offered a tempting target, controlling as they did hundreds of thousands of acres of the best land and having 42,000 cattle, 3000 horses, and 210,000 sheep and goats. The farms all tended to be very large and isolated, and were thus hardly defensible. In all, there were only 267 farms in the northern part of the colony. The Hereros reasoned that the colonial government existed largely for the sake of those several dozen farms. If the settlers became discouraged and left the land, Samuel believed that the rest of the Germans would also pack up and leave. But Samuel feared that a general attack on defenseless civilians might easily lead to an orgy of wanton killing, and this he wanted to avoid at all costs.

The Germans found this unexpected streak of humanity hard to understand, but looked at from the Herero point of view it is not really so baffling. In the first place Samuel was a Christian, and he owed his position as Paramount Chief in part to the influence of the Rhenish mission who supported him over his non-Christian rivals. While it was true that he had been put under censure by the Church and that he had no rights in the congregation, he held to his faith, such as it was, even though it raised a serious question in the eyes of many Hereros whether he could perform the religious duties incumbent on a paramount chief. Beyond religious considerations, Samuel was no doubt influenced by plain self-interest, but whatever his reason he issued a strikingly unequivocal manifesto on the eve of the revolt, in which he declared: "I am the principal chief of the Hereros. I have proclaimed the law and the just word, and I mean for all my people. They should not lay hands on any of the following: Englishmen, Basters, Berg Damaras, Namas, and Boers. On none of these shall hands be laid. I have pledged my honor that this thing shall not take place. Nor shall the missionaries be harmed. Enough!"[23] In addition, he prohibited the killing of women and children. Militarily Samuel's prohibitions make good sense. By not molesting the Boers and the English he reduced the number of his enemies and held open the possibility of British assistance in the event the rebellion sparked a colonial war in South Africa. As for the Namas (that is, the Hottentots) the Berg Damaras, and Basters, they had been traditional enemies of the Hereros, but as in the case of the British and the Boers, Samuel wanted to reduce the number of his enemies and create the basis for possible cooperation against the Germans in the future. As for the missionaries, Samuel himself was a Christian, but more than that he knew that the missionaries had considerable influence in Germany, and he hoped that they would plead the Hereros' case in Germany, which indeed they did. His remarkable order, then, can easily be interpreted as an example of enlightened self-interest, but

23. Quoted in Drechsler, *Südwestafrika*, pp. 166-167. See also Leutwein, *Elf Jahre*, p. 467.

the tone of the order and the scrupulous way in which it was carried out, plus the fact that the order was in direct conflict with the traditional Herero way of making war, suggest that something further was in Samuel's mind. From the missionaries and from the colonial officials he had been taught that he was a "barbarian" and that they were "civilized." One of the most commonly cited proofs of the barbarism of the native was their manner of carrying on war—with indiscriminate slaughter of prisoners, massacres of women and children, torture, cruelty, and unrestrained sadism. Samuel seemed to have had some historic sense that in this moment of destiny he must meet and surpass the standards of civilization as defined by the Germans.

In addition to attacking the German farms, Samuel also ordered a general attack on the German outposts. Though most of the German towns were at least harassed in the first week of the rebellion, only two or three minor outposts suffered more than discomfort. In no case was a major fortress attacked. At most the railroad lines were cut, telegraph lines torn down, and a passive siege set up. Why was more energetic action not taken, particularly against Windhoek, which was all but defenseless and contained significant quantities of guns and ammunition? Several answers can be given. In the first place, the Hereros had no equipment for breaching walls. Second, the Germans could maximize their advantage in firepower when they were protected behind thick walls and firing against Herero warriors in the open. Finally, the Hereros seemed to have a deep-seated aversion to fighting in and among towns and fortresses.

Beyond attacking the farms and towns, Samuel tried to enlist the support of the other natives in South West Africa under the slogan "Africa for Africans." We have indirect evidence that he made some contact with the Ovambo, because they did attack a German fort on their frontier in the first days of the revolt; but we have no other evidence of any contact. As for the Hottentots, we have direct evidence of Samuel's diplomacy in action. In the weeks before the outbreak of the rebellion Samuel wrote a number of letters to the various Orlam and Hottentot chiefs, pleading with them to join him in a common front against the Germans. To the Baster Chief Hermanus van Wyk, Samuel wrote: "I would rather that they [the Germans] annihilate us and take over our lands than to go on as we are." Hermanus, however, remained adamant in his support of the Germans. He sent a force of scouts to assist the Germans, and his loyalty was rewarded, for the Basters survived the holocaust that engulfed most of the rest of the natives.

To the redoubtable Hendrik Witbooi, the leader of the Hottentots and long-time foe of the Hereros, Samuel wrote: "All our obedience and patience with the Germans avails us nothing. My brother, do not go back on your word and stay out of the fighting, but rather let all the people fight against the Germans and let us be resolved to die together rather than to be killed by the Germans through mistreatment, imprisonment, or some other way. Further, you should inform all your captains who are subject to you that they too should stand and fight."[24] The wording of the letter suggests that Samuel had already made some sort of agreement with Hendrik Witbooi, but of this prior agreement we know nothing. In a letter to the son of Chief Zacharias of Otjimbingwe (the same man whose wife had been murdered by a white man a few months before) Samuel summed up his position with great eloquence: "Your father knows that if we rebel we will be annihilated in battle since our people are practically unarmed and without ammunition, but the cruelty and injustice of the Germans have driven us to despair and our leaders and our people both feel that death has lost its terrors because of the conditions under which we now live." Samuel's letters to other Herero chiefs, for the most part, reached their destination, but his letters to the Hottentots, which were sent by way of the Basters, were turned over to the Germans by Hermanus van Wyk. Just what Hendrik Witbooi would have done had he received the letters is not clear, but as it was, the uprising, or at least its precise date, must have been as much a surprise to him as it was to the Germans.

In the days immediately preceding January 12, 1904, there were numerous reports from all over Hereroland of a growing state of excitement and tension. Oddly enough, until the last

24. Drechsler, *Südwestafrika*, p. 166.

possible moment few Germans believed that all this activity
was the harbinger of any sort of mass action against their rule.
At most, the Germans believed that some minor disturbance
(which on balance most whites welcomed) was in the offing.
Traders reported that blacks were buying horses and equipage
regardless of price; many whites told of a marked increase in
incidents of "cheekiness" on the part of their servants.[25] At
Okahandja a large number of armed Hereros rode through the
town on the night of January 11-12, 1904, much to the consternation of the inhabitants. In the absence of Leutwein, command of the German forces passed to a civilian official named
Duft. Alarmed by the growing signs of Herero unrest, Duft,
accompanied by 20 soldiers, went by train from Windhoek to
Okahandja on January 11. His intention was to talk to the
Herero chiefs then encamped near the town, in the hope of
persuading them to return to their werfts. His intentions in
themselves stand as a revealing commentary on his own judgment of the situation.

On January 12, 1904, the Hereros launched their first attacks.
During the next ten days almost every farm, village, and fort in
Hereroland was attacked or at least threatened by marauding
bands of natives. The majority of the German farms were
destroyed during those hectic days. By January 20, in the Windhoek area alone civilian casualties had reached thirteen. Of that
number six were farmers; one a farm hand; two surveyors; two
merchants; one a policeman; and one a 14-year-old boy. No
women or children had been killed. Of those farmers who
survived all had fled to Windhoek and in most cases they had
lost everything: their livestock had been stolen; their possessions looted, and their buildings burned. In addition, all the
major fortified places in Hereroland—including Omaruru, Otjimbingwe, Okahandja, Gobabis, Outjo, and Windhoek—were
loosely besieged, though no fortified place fallen. Despite the
loss of the countryside the garrisons were in no immediate
danger, but as Leutwein noted later, those who lived through
those nerve-shattering days, completely cut off as they were

25. *Official History*, I, 24.

from the outside world, found it hard to comprehend that they were in no real danger. In all somewhere between 123 (Leutwein's figure) and 150 (Wellington's figure) died. Of that number, seven were Boers and three were women. Of the deaths of the women, Leutwein noted that "you will always find a few monsters." Tales of castrated children were common at the time and reprinted in the semi-official *Kolonialblatt*, but subsequent investigation failed to confirm any of these horror stories.

We have one extremely interesting document concerning the Hererros' action during these first days. A woman named Else Sonnenberg lived with her husband at Waterberg, where they ran a general store. By Christmas she noted that the Hereros were on a major buying spree, and when her husband tried to reduce credit buying they laughed at him. On January 13 several Hereros came to her house and inquired after her husband; she told them he was sleeping, whereupon they forced their way in and bludgeoned him to death. Two weeks later Frau Sonnenberg was ordered by the local Herero chieftain to get ready to be taken to Okahandja. Together with a missionary and his wife, Frau Sonnenberg was taken by slow stages to the south. In mid-February the group reached Okaharui, where they observed a large Herero encampment which Frau Sonnenberg believed to have consisted of 20,000 or more natives. A few days later Herero guides released their prisoners in the vicinity of Okahandja, exhausted and shaken but unharmed.

On January 14, 1904, the German government and people received the first news of the outbreak. A Wolff Bureau telegram reported: "The Hereros have opened hostilities, besieging Okahandja and destroying the railroad bridge at Osona about three kilometers southeast of Okahandja and cutting the telegraph connection with Windhoek." Each subsequent day brought new reports from South West Africa, and for many weeks the news was all bad. The immediate response was one of disbelief, followed closely by demands for vengeance. On January 18, Bülow addressed the Reichstag on the situation in South West Africa, which he conceded was serious. He argued that the uprising was totally unexpected even by the experts, and he added that it was "without apparent cause." Since the governor and most of the colonial forces were twenty days' march to the south, Bülow said that he had ordered the immediate dispatch of a company of Marine infantry and he requested that the house vote credit which would pay for the sending of 500 men, six machine guns, and six artillery pieces in early February. He concluded his statement by saying he was confident all Germans would unite "to defend the honor of the flag." The next day the Colonial Minister, Stübel, gave the House more specific details about the troubles in South West Africa. He confirmed Bülow's statement that the uprising was a complete surprise, but he did suggest a possible cause. The Hereros, he noted, still remembered the days before German rule, when they were completely free, and it was to regain that freedom that they had revolted. The leader of the Social Democrats, Bebel, countered these assertions with a call for a complete investigation into the causes. Bebel left no doubt that in his opinion it was the whites and particularly the traders who had driven the Hereros to revolt.

The response of the Germans in the colony was rather like that of their fellow countrymen in the homeland, but their shock was understandably greater and their thirst for vengeance more untempered. "The uprising was completely unexpected by the government," wrote Leutwein, "and by the missionaries and settlers. In a way which we held to be impossible the Hereros concealed their intentions from us completely. . . . It was a real Sicilian Vespers. I had intimate contact with the Hereros for over ten years and came to believe that I understood them, but I would never have thought it possible for them to mount such a coordinated, energetic effort."

The Siege of Okahandja and Windhoek

Okahandja and Windhoek were the two principal towns in Hereroland. Had the Germans lost them, the problem of reestablishing control over the colony would have been multiplied many times. Windhoek (from the Dutch meaning windy corner) was located almost exactly in the center of the colony and was actually south of the traditional Herero grazing areas,

although from time to time in the nineteenth century the Hereros moved into the area. As the administrative center of the
colony, Windhoek boasted a number of substantial buildings
including the government house, the financial office, a hospital, a school, and two churches. The population at the time of
the outbreak was about 1000 whites and rather fewer natives.
There was a small fort built by von François in the early 1890's,
but the town itself was widely dispersed and not easily defensible. Beyond its role as the symbol of German rule, Windhoek
was also the site of the colony's major magazines, in which were
stored large quantities of guns and ammunition. Okahandja
was rather different, for in 1903 it was still basically a native
town. The white population was only 159, while over 1000
natives lived in and around the town, including Samuel Maharero.[26] The fortress at Okahandja was a massive structure
with imposing walls and four large watchtowers guarding the
four corners of the fort. In the first hours of the revolt, both
towns were subject to attack.

During the night of January 10-11 a large group of Hereros
rode through Okahandja and camped a few miles to the southwest near the railroad bridge at Osona. That same night Samuel
Maharero disappeared. The district chief, a man named Zürn,
was sufficiently alarmed by these events to send a wire to
Leutwein's deputy, Bergrat Duft, in Windhoek. Duft, not suspecting that Windhoek was in any danger, left at once for
Okahandja by train. He took with him twenty soldiers, which
was most of the remaining Windhoek garrison. When Duft
arrived at Okahandja he found the people there nervously
preparing for a possible attack by the Hereros, who were encamped a few miles from the town. Duft tried to contact Samuel
Maharero but was unable to do so. He did, however, succeed in
making contact with a minor chief, Ouanja from Otjikurume,
who assured Duft that the gathering of the Herero warriors was
perfectly harmless. Neither Duft nor Zürn believed this, and
they pushed forward with the task of preparing the fort for a

26. In 1903 the town had an estimated population of 1250. Of that
number 159 were white, 900 Herero, 100 Berg Damaras, and 100 Hottentots.

siege. Duft ordered a patrol to ride to the north and warn the farmers there that trouble was imminent. At some time in the next several days the patrol was ambushed and all its members killed. Late in the afternoon of January 11 Duft walked out of the fort alone to see for himself what the situation was. He was warned by an old Herero to turn back, but undeterred he strolled into the countryside. What he saw thoroughly alarmed him. Around Samuel's house was a large group of mounted men who had a distinctly unfriendly air about them, and in the hills around the town he could plainly make out a large number of Herero warriors.

On the morning of January 12, 1904, the Hereros rode into the town and proceeded to loot the stores, burn several buildings, and kill a few civilians who failed to take refuge in the fort. The town was lost to the Hereros, who held it until January 28. The Hereros also destroyed the railroad bridge at Osona and cut the telegraph lines that linked the town with Windhoek and Swakopmund. By cutting the Swakopmund line they also cut the colony off from the outside world. Just before the line was cut, however, Zürn managed to get out one vital message to the commander of Swakopmund harbor, alerting him to the danger and calling for assistance. Between January 12 and 15 the fortress was completely cut off from the outside. Though the Hereros made no serious attempt to storm the fortress, they did beat back a sortie. On January 15, 1904, the first relief arrived. A Lieutenant Zülow, with a hastily put-together company of reserves, had left Swakopmund within hours after Zürn's call for help. Zülow and his force of 100 men had reached Karibib without incident. After seeing to it that the town was in condition to repel an attack, Zülow pushed on to Okahandja. Despite the fact that the tracks were in several places destroyed—in part because of hostile action, in part because of the habitual maintenance problems—Zülow had no choice but to stay on the railroad because he was bringing, in addition to reinforcements, 50,000 rounds of ammunition and a large supply of food.

On January 15 Zülow's train crossed the Osona bridge, which was still intact, and arrived at Okahandja without any serious interference. Zülow, as the senior officer in the besieged fortress (Zürn was a lieutenant in the reserves), took command. On January 19, 1904, he sent out an armored train in the direction of Windhoek to examine the condition of the track. Before the train had gone more than a short distance from the town, the crew discovered a 200-yard-long strip of destroyed track. The troops on the train were then ordered into the town and surrounding area to recover any military stores missed by the Hereros. There they found a few guns, some ammunition, and a stock of dynamite. The next day Zülow sent the train out in the direction of Karibib. Some miles from Okahandja the train was again stopped by a long section of destroyed track; this time when the soldiers got off the train they were met by an ambush in which four were killed and four more seriously wounded. In the days following, Zülow sent out repeated patrols to reconnoitre, to discover the position and intentions of the enemy, and to establish contact with any possible relief columns. Finally, on January 28, 1904 (the Kaiser's birthday), Captain Franke and the Second Company arrived and drove the Hereros away from the immediate vicinity of Okahandja. The total German losses were fifteen dead and about the same number wounded. Almost all these casualties were sustained by German troops outside the walls of the fort.

The situation in Windhoek was rather different than in Okahandja. Samuel had planned to take the town and its stores, but when he received no word from Hendrik Witbooi that the Hottentots would cooperate, Samuel may have modified his orders. This much is clear: Windhoek had fewer troops, a less imposing fortress, and was of more value to the Hereros than Okahandja. Still, no serious effort was made to take the town. On January 12, 1904, farms all around Windhoek were attacked by Hereros led by Frederick Maharero, the son of Samuel. Within the town a volunteer force of 70 men was raised that day, but whether the buildings outside the fort could be defended was at best doubtful. On the night of January 15 the Hereros did attack several outposts around the town and were driven off with some losses. Perhaps this action discouraged Frederick, but for whatever reason, the attack was not pressed

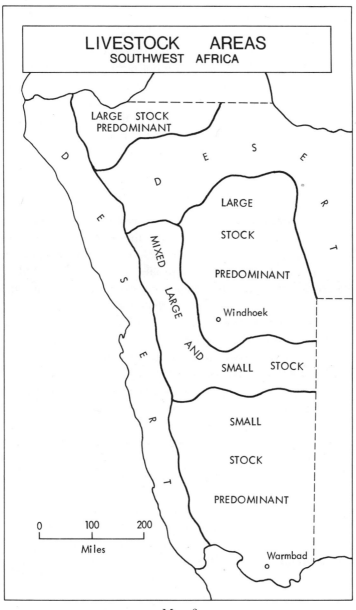

LIVESTOCK AREAS
SOUTHWEST AFRICA

LARGE STOCK
PREDOMINANT

DESERT

LARGE

STOCK

PREDOMINANT

Windhoek

MIXED LARGE AND

SMALL STOCK

SMALL

STOCK

PREDOMINANT

0   100   200
Miles

Warmbad

Map 3

home. One interesting possibility is the oft-repeated assertion that Hereros had a deep-set prejudice against fighting in built-up areas, not because of the danger, but because they considered it unmanly.[27] Whether this prejudice is sufficient to explain the failure to attack Windhoek is a moot point, but it is undoubtedly the case that the failure to attack was a critical error. Never again did the Hereros have such a superb opportunity to solve their logistic problems, particularly in regard to ammunition, and at the same time deal a blow to German prestige which might well have been sufficient to rouse the other tribes.

The German Response

After the initial shock wore off, the Germans moved to regain the initiative. Two tasks were of prime importance: first, to repair the railroad line, and second, to establish contact with the outlying stations. The extent and fury of the initial blow effectively immobilized such German troops as were stationed in Hereroland, so until reinforcements could be found there was little hope of improving the situation. Fortunately for the Germans, two relief units were available for service in Herero-land: a landing party from the German gunboat *Habicht*, and the Fourth Company, commanded by Captain Franke, which was on the march to the south when the first news of the uprising was received. On January 14 the German naval high command ordered the *Habicht*, which was then in Capetown, to proceed under full steam for Swakopmund and render such assistance as might be necessary. On the afternoon of January 18 the gunboat steamed into Swakopmund, and the commanding officer put his men to work immediately to restore service on the railroad. Their task was formidable. Twenty engines were at the moment out of commission, not because of enemy action but because of poor maintenance; the roadbed was washed out at several places; the Hereros had destroyed several sections of track; and the bridge at Osona had been burned. Despite the

27. During the entire war the Hereros never did fight any action in a built-up area.

wretched condition of the equipment and tracks, and in the face of enemy harassment, the sailors worked with remarkable speed and by early February the line was open as far as Okahandja.

While the landing party of the *Habicht* was working on the railroad, the Fourth Company was heading north by forced marches. When the first reports of trouble were received, Leutwein ordered Captain Franke to turn around and march back to Windhoek.[28] After the first day's march, Franke learned that the situation in Hereroland was much worse than he had originally supposed. Assuming the worst, he called his men together and addressed them as follows (the account is taken from the daybook of a trooper who was present): "I have reports that a serious fight has taken place in the vicinity of Windhoek and that no news has come through from Okahandja. Today I had only planned to go as far as Kuis, but now it is clear that we must go further. I must demand from every man, whether trooper or officer, the utmost!" Two days later the column reached Windhoek, having covered close to 200 miles in the preceding 100 hours. The official German history waxed poetic over Franke's "epic" march which, they wrote, "taught anew how far men can surpass the boundaries of human endurance when a strong and unbendable will rules."[29]

Upon reaching Windhoek, Franke found that the reports of fierce fighting were greatly exaggerated. True, the Hereros had burned most of the farmhouses in the vicinity of the town and driven off all the cattle, but they had made no move to attack the fortress itself and did not seem much inclined to do so. Seeing that Windhoek was more or less secure, Franke pushed on to Okahandja. On reaching Osona, high water temporarily prevented the column from fording the Swakop River. It was not until January 27—the day before the Kaiser's birthday—that Franke and his men marched into Okahandja, to the immense relief of the townspeople and the garrison. As at Windhoek, it was apparent that the fortress of Okahandja was relatively safe, so Franke again pushed on, this time his goal

28. See *Official History*, I, 35-58, for a full account.
29 *Ibid.*, I, 37.

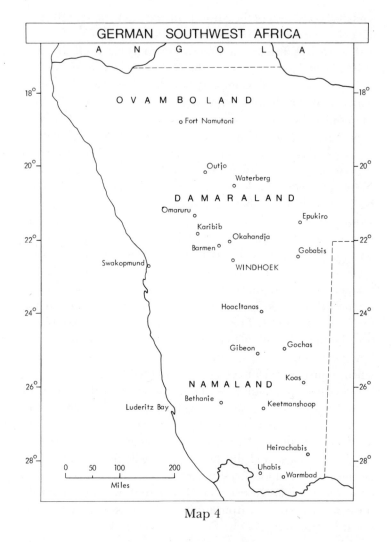

Map 4

being Omaruru, where only a few weeks before he had been stationed as district officer. As the Fourth Company neared Omaruru they were met by a large body of Hereros, many of whom Franke recognized. As their movements suggested hostility, Franke decided to bring them to their senses by showing himself to his former subjects in the hope that his presence would have a sobering influence on them. Accordingly, he

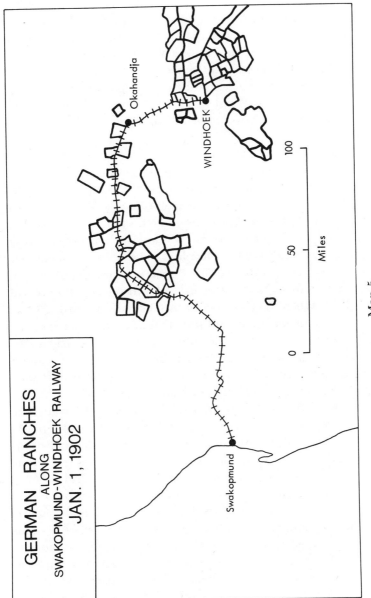

GERMAN RANCHES
ALONG
SWAKOPMUND-WINDHOEK RAILWAY
JAN. 1, 1902

Okahandja

WINDHOEK

Swakopmund

Miles

0   50   100

Map 5

donned a pure white uniform, mounted his own white horse, and rode out before his restive subjects. The Hereros were unimpressed and greeted his appearance with a hail of bullets. A lively fire-fight ensued in which the Hereros were bested and forced to withdraw and leave the way to Omaruru open. The costs of this first pitched battle of the campaign were, for the Germans, disconcertingly high: six men were killed and another fifteen were wounded out of a force of less than one hundred.

After Franke's "great ride" the situation in Hereroland was, for the moment at least, stabilized. The rebels had been driven away from the major German forts, and communication between most of the outlying garrisons had been re-established. There was also good news from the north and south. At Fort Namutoni a German sergeant and four men had been trapped in the watchtower of the fort by a force of 600 Ovambos. The five Germans poured a deadly accurate fire down upon the "rampaging natives," who were armed for the most part only with spears. When the battle ended the Germans counted 108 dead Ovambo in and around the fort. This one action convinced the Ovambo, few of whom had guns, that it would be madness for them to take any further part in the uprising. In the south, Leutwein patched up a hurried peace with the Bondelzwarts and headed north to take personal command of the situation. On February 11, 1904, he arrived at Swakopmund, having come by sea. Leutwein's first reaction had been to minimize the seriousness of the situation, but after being briefed at Swakopmund he had to admit that the Herero uprising was very serious indeed. He conceded that the Hereros in a month had destroyed the whole structure of German order so painfully built up in the preceding decade. Though he admitted the full gravity of the situation, Leutwein believed that the most effective action would be to mark time while exploring possible diplomatic openings. As a preliminary step, he sent a letter to his old friend Samuel Maharero asking him to agree to a parley.

In Berlin, German colonial officials were outraged when they learned that Leutwein had stooped to making what they considered to be a "premature" peace offer. In the view of German officialdom, German prestige had suffered such a blow that only a total military victory could restore it. Accordingly, Leutwein was ordered to cease and desist all communication with the enemy. Leutwein tried to justify his attempts to contact Samuel in a letter which read in part: "My letter [to Samuel] contained no proposals which were in any way binding and its only purpose was to ascertain—in the safest way possible— whether the reports that the majority of the Hereros are in the vicinity of the Otjisongati copper mine were true or not. This method of learning the location of the enemy has been used by me before with success for it assures that there are no losses on patrol."[30] Even after receiving this explanation, Leutwein's superiors in the colonial department remained unimpressed and ordered him to get on with the business of defeating the Hereros at once. Leutwein protested that unless some hope of a negotiated peace was held out to the Hereros they would have no alternative but to fight to the death, but even this argument was of no avail and his orders to fight as soon as possible remained unaltered.

Ordered by the government in Berlin to insist on unconditional surrender, Leutwein answered in a letter which is of considerable importance because it demonstrates very clearly the harshness of even the most advanced of the colonial officials:

> In colonial questions the diplomat must always stand next to the leader. The rebels must know that a line of retreat is open to them which does not in every case lead to death. Otherwise we will drive them to desperation and the war will end in a fashion which will be to our disadvantage. For the enemy will have nothing to lose other than his life which would already be forfeited while we, because our colonization has come to a standstill, must suffer a daily loss. For example, the Spanish continuously won "victories" in Cuba, but they did not succeed in bringing the war to an end and consequently lost the island.
>
> I agree with the authorities in Berlin that the future conditions of subjection should be such that there should be for the Hereros after all their misdeeds nothing but unconditional sur-

30. Drechsler, *Südwestafrika*, p. 172.

render. On the other hand I must say that I do not agree with those strident voices raised in favor of total annihilation of the Hereros. Aside from the fact that a people numbering 60,000 to 70,000 cannot be so easily annihilated, I would have to argue that such a measure would be an economic error. We need the Hereros as herdsmen and as workers. The people must only suffer a political death. When this is in some measure realized they will no longer possess a tribal government and they must be confined to reserves which will just suffice for their needs. . . .

Even those villages which did not participate must be disarmed and submit to confinement on reserves. Some prisoners of war will be remanded to military courts and, in case they are found guilty of plundering farms or murdering their inhabitants, they must be punished with death. These outrageous misdeeds deserve no other punishment. Moreover before any definite settlement is made I will gladly refer the matter to the higher authorities. Only in connection with the diplomatic means to be used up to the conclusion of the agreement do I ask to be given a free hand.[31]

If Leutwein found little support for his relatively moderate approach in Berlin, he found even less in the colony itself. "The most severe punishment of the enemy is necessary," advised the captain of the *Habicht* a few days after he arrived in South West Africa, and this same sentiment was repeated over and over again by settlers, officers, and officials in the colony. The military commander of Swakopmund telegraphed the Foreign Office on January 19, 1904, recommending that "the Hereros be disarmed, ruthlessly punished, and made to do forced labor on the railroads."[32] The chief engineer of the Otavi construction company was writing at the same time that "everyone here believes that the uprising must be smashed ruthlessly and a tabula rasa created."[33] A missionary who was generally sympathetic to the Hereros reported: "The Germans are filled with fearful hate and a frightful thirst for revenge, I must really call it a blood thirst, against the Hereros. One hears nothing but talk of 'cleaning up,' 'executing,' 'shooting down to the last man,' 'no pardon,' etc. It frightens me to think of the next

---

31. *Ibid.*, pp. 172-173.   32. *Ibid.*, p. 168.   33. *Ibid.*

months. The Germans will undoubtedly take a fearful revenge."[34]

During the months of February and March, 1576 officers and
men, 10 pieces of artillery, 6 machine guns, and 1000 horses
arrived in South West Africa to reinforce the German troops
there. With the arrival of these fresh troops Leutwein was able
to put an army of 2500 men in the field to confront 10,000
Hereros, many of whom were unarmed. Despite the massive
German superiority in firepower, it was the Hereros who grew
stronger in the weeks that followed the first attacks. Their
marksmen grew more accurate, their captains more resourceful,
their stocks of weapons and ammunition more plentiful, and
their determination fed by desperation grew more adamant.
Surprise was gone, numerical superiority was gone (by March
there were more *armed* Germans in South West Africa than
armed Hereros), and equipment shortages remained, but the
Hereros managed to retain the initiative. They determined when
and where the battles would be fought. The timorousness of the
Germans led the Hereros to believe that the Germans were too
cowardly to fight in the open; the black warriors asked their
prisoners contemptuously whether the almighty soldiers of the
Kaiser dared to fight anywhere except "behind walls."

The temporary decline in the effectiveness of the German
forces, despite their steadily increasing numbers, was hard for
the armchair generals in Berlin to comprehend, although to the
officers on the spot it was perfectly understandable. The colonial army at the outbreak of the rebellion was an excellent military organization. It was highly mobile and capable of operating for long periods of time far from its bases. Both its officers
and men knew the country well, and the commanders had
adjusted their tactical and strategic ideas to the realities of the
land. The German troops were both lean and tough, as the ride
of Captain Franke's Fourth Company had demonstrated. With
the arrival of reinforcements, encumbered as they were with the
baggage, both mental and material, of the Imperial army, the

34. *Ibid.*, p. 169.

veterans quickly became part of a cumbersome bureaucratic
system that destroyed both their mobility and much of their
initiative.

The Hereros

The German response to the initial attack is both well docu-
mented and perfectly consistent with what we know about
European military thinking at the time. As for the Hereros, we
have very little evidence that sheds any light on their evaluation
of the situation after the first few days, or how they planned to
exploit the temporarily favorable position in which they found
themselves. We do know that the actions of those days fused the
tribe into a cohesive force such as it had never been before.[35] No
longer was the old German strategy of divide and conquer
effective. The fact that Samuel Maharero put himself at the
head of the rebellion was no doubt a factor, for he was the
richest and most powerful of the Herero chiefs and had inher-
ited from his father and grandfather something close to over-
lordship over the Herero tribes. Another factor was unques-
tionably raw, naked fear. After the initial rampage, every Herero assumed, and rightly so, that the tribe as a whole would be
held accountable for the violence and that all would be punished whether they had had any hand in those outrages or not.
But beyond fear, many Hereros joined the fighting out of a
sense of loyalty to their tribe. Nearly one-third of the 900
Hereros working in South Africa left the mines in the spring of
1904 and returned to take part in the rebellion. As they were
under no compulsion of any kind, their actions must have been
prompted by a feeling of tribal unity.

Given that the tribe was unified and under the command of
Samuel Maharero, is it possible to discern any pattern in the
actions of the Hereros in the period after the initial attacks and
before the Germans took the offensive for the first time in

35. The missionary Kuhlmann, who visited the Herero camp during
this time, was impressed by the control that Samuel exercised over the
subordinate chiefs. By June, when the Hereros were encamped at
Waterberg, their unity of purpose had begun to crumble.

March? This was, of course, a critical period. The advantage lay with the Hereros. The German accounts imply that the Hereros spent those critical weeks in aimless plundering and looting, but if we take the reported moves of the Hereros it is possible to see something other than this—to see, in fact, the outline of a tactically sound scheme.

Up to January 28, 1904, the Hereros had free run throughout their former ancestral homeland. During this period there is little evidence of a coherent plan of action beyond the fact that each group took as much as it could. There was nothing to fear from the German soldiers, since they were all cowering behind the walls of the forts, and still less from the German farmers, since they were either dead or had abandoned their farms for the safety of the forts. Almost every fort and station was "besieged" during these days, but that word probably gives a false impression of the situation. It is true that there were Herero bands in the vicinity of every fort, but in no case was any attempt made to storm a fortification, and the Hereros knew that for all practical purposes the well-stocked German forts could not be starved out. So the siege consisted of nothing more than a Herero force in the immediate vicinity of each station, with the apparent duty of watching the Germans to insure that they did not try to prevent destruction of the neighboring farms. It should be noted that a number of women and children were allowed by the Hereros through their lines into the towns, and also that the Herero in command of the forces near Okahandja offered to allow all women and children to leave the fort and return to Germany.

By the end of January the temporary superiority of the Hereros had ended with the arrival of Captain Franke and the Fourth Company, together with a landing party from the *Habicht*. Several minor fire-fights (particularly the one at Omaruru) convinced Samuel that it would be impossible to prevent the Germans from opening the railroad and establishing lines of communication between the various posts. The firepower of the Germans was simply too great. Samuel therefore decided to withdraw from the vicinity of the railroad. Looking back on it, this seems a strange decision. Without the railroad the Germans could never have maintained their position in South West Africa. And the railroad was particularly vulnerable to guerrilla warfare. Samuel knew the vital significance of the railroad, and yet he abandoned any serious attempt to prevent its reopening after the end of January. One might argue that he made a simple mistake, but it would seem more reasonable to search for some other explanation, for Samuel was not given to making crude military errors.

In all likelihood, Samuel's decision was based on three factors. In the first place, his warriors had captured several thousand head of cattle, and the security of this plunder was an important consideration; it could best be protected by withdrawing from the immediate vicinity of German power, where the chances of losing the newly acquired herds were too great. Secondly, Samuel, like any general, wanted to protect his line of retreat, and that line was in the direction of Bechuanaland to the east. If worse came to worst, he kept open the possibility of escaping over the border into English territory. The Germans feared that this is what he had in mind, and settlers asked the government to prevent Maharero's escape with their cattle. Because the railroad lay to the west, to have harassed it would have made an escape to the east just that much more difficult. Finally, Maharero doubtless reasoned that after the arrival of reinforcements any further offensive action on his part was doomed to failure because of the firepower of the Germans, but that if he retreated into hills where the Germans would have to fight on ground of his choosing, he would still have more than an even chance of inflicting such losses on the Germans that they might tire of the game and leave South West Africa.

As soon as Franke arrived the Hereros began to disappear from the vicinity of the forts and drift into the bush. By the time Leutwein arrived on February 11, 1904, to take command of the operations, he was unsure where the main body of the Hereros was encamped. His initial move was to send a messenger to Samuel asking him to parlay. Leutwein explained this action to his indignant superiors in Berlin as a ruse to help him locate Samuel, but the explanation seems forced. Samuel must have assumed that Leutwein's position was serious and that he knew it. Of course, Samuel knew as well as anyone that if the Germans wanted to conquer South West Africa they had the power to do so; but he also knew that the cost would be high and that even a total military victory would not restore the economy.

By the end of February the bulk of the Hereros were in the Onjati hills. Three relatively small groups were separated from the main body: one was south of the railroad, a second to the west of Waterberg, and a third far to the east near Gobabis. Leutwein undertook to attack these in detail, but he succeeded only in driving them toward the Onjati hills, where in all probability they were heading anyway.

4

The March and April Disasters

DURING THE MONTHS of March and April Leutwein reluctantly undertook the task of trying to force the Hereros to fight in the open, because his superiors in Berlin were convinced that German firepower would be decisive. As a result of this misguided policy, the Imperial German Army suffered the indignity of being repeatedly defeated by what Europeans regarded as a handful of half-naked black men. In those golden days of the white man's burden, no major power would have endured this trial with equanimity, least of all the Germans. Those Herero victories, glorious as they were at the time, sealed the fate of the tribe, for they convinced the military authorities in Berlin that nothing short of total annihilation would be acceptable. In terms of human suffering it would have been far better had the Hereros been beaten down at the very beginning, for then the German *amour propre* would not have been involved, and the conquerors might have been inclined to display a shred of generosity to a defeated foe.

Leutwein's plan clearly mirrored all of his doubts about the wisdom of forcing a premature action.[1] His objectives as outlined in his operation order were diverse and to some extent contradictory. His first interest was to establish firm and unbroken contact with all of the outlying garrisons. Next, he

1. *Official History*, I, 62.

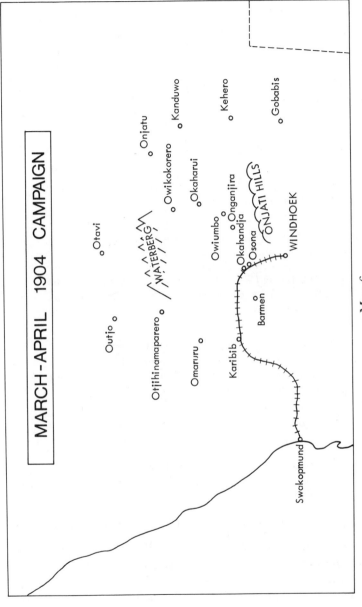

MARCH-APRIL 1904 CAMPAIGN

Otavi

Outjo

Otjihinamaparero

Omaruru

WATERBERG

Owikokorero

Onjatu

Kanduwo

Okaharui

Kehero

Gobabis

Owiumbo

Onganjira

Okahandja

Osona

ONJATI HILLS

WINDHOEK

Karibib

Barmen

Swakopmund

Map 6

thought it would be advantageous to drive the enemy out of the area south of the railroad in order to give a greater measure of security to his only link with the outside world. Furthermore, in deference to the clamor of the colonists, he agreed to try to prevent the exodus of the main body of the Hereros into British territory so that the tens of thousands of head of stolen cattle would not be permanently lost. Finally, he wanted to keep the various groups of Herero warriors separated so that he could defeat them piecemeal. To carry out these varied objectives Leutwein divided his forces into three sections: the West Section under Major von Estorff; the East Section under Major Glasenapp; and the Main Section which he himself commanded. The forces assigned to each section were as follows:

1. East Section
   Company von Winkler (Eighth Field Company)
   Company Eggers (Ninth Field Company)
   Company Fischel (First Company Marine Infantry)
   Company Lieber (Fourth Company Marine Infantry)
   Two field pieces; four rapid-fire guns; one revolver gun; two machine guns.

2. West Section
   Company Franke (Second Field Company)
   Company von Schönau (Fourth Field Company)
   Company Haering (Third Company Marine Infantry)
   Four field pieces; one mountain gun; two machine guns.

3. Main Section
   Company Count Stillfried (First Field Company)
   Company Puder (Fifth Field Company)
   Company von Bagenski (Sixth Field Company)
   Company Schering (Second Company Marine Infantry)
   Battery von Oertzen (First Field Battery, four 5.7 cm guns)
   Battery von Heydebreck (Second Mountain Battery, 3 mountain guns)
   Battery Bauszus (Third Field Battery, four 5.7 cm guns)

Leutwein ordered Major Estorff's West Section to clear the Hereros from the vicinity of Omaruru and, after having accomplished this, to establish contact with the garrison at Outjo. The East Section was to join forces with the garrison at Gobabis and together they were to close the eastern frontier to prevent any Hereros from crossing into Bechuanaland. For himself

Leutwein reserved the task of securing the railroad and then defeating the Herero main force, which was believed to be located somewhere to the northeast in the Onjati mountains.

From the beginning the operations did not go well, largely because the new troops were quite unprepared for the rigors of desert warfare. The Hereros were amazed at the poor quality of the new arrivals, whom they referred to as "boys" in contrast to the "men" who made up the original colonial force. The officers, all of whom had to have excellent connections to get a chance to fight in South West Africa, landed at Swakopmund apparently under the impression they were going on a glorified big game hunt. Von Deimling, who was later to command all the German forces in South West Africa, described his feeling when he heard that large-scale fighting had broken out: "My soldier's blood was agitated. For thirty years I had served in the peacetime army either in the field or in the "big building" in Berlin [the Great General Staff], and during that time I had thought through all the aspects of war. I knew very well, however, that the real test of my profession was to face the enemy in the field."[2] Veterans reported with dismay that the newly arrived officers were fully supplied with vintage champagnes, their favorite cigars, and hunting rifles.

Not only were the new arrivals ill-prepared for serious fighting, but the communication equipment of the German army, upon which the coordination of large-scale operations depended, was nearly useless in South West Africa. The standard means of communication in the German army, the telegraph, was of little value in a hostile land where no area was secure unless soldiers were actually guarding it. Wireless equipment was not available in 1904, so Germans were forced to use heliographs when telegraph lines were not available. These heliographs were both secure and reasonably effective, but also very scarce. The result of this lack of communication equipment was that when the East and West Sections parted from Leutwein they disappeared into a void for several weeks. There

2. B. von Deimling, *Aus alten Zeiten in die neue Zeit: Lebesnerin-nerungen* (Berlin, 1930), p. 27.

was no chance for Leutwein to change his orders, nor any way to coordinate their movements with those of the Main Section. Besides the deficiency in communication equipment, the very firepower of the German army was in many ways a disadvantage. A machine gun can expend several hundred pounds of ammunition in an hour; a 5.7 rapid-fire field piece can shoot 5 shells each weighing 25 pounds in a minute; a standard German army repeating rifle in the hands of untrained men had a voracious appetite for ammunition. Thus the German columns were slowed by the necessity of hauling heavy ammunition wagons through a country without roads, so that the firepower of the Germans was bought at the cost of mobility. Given the handicaps under which the Germans operated in those harrowing weeks in March and April, they were lucky that they were not defeated more decisively than they were.

The West Section

Major Estorff with the West Section had what turned out to be the easiest task, and he was the only one of the three section commanders who could claim even a partial success. On February 20, 1904, Estorff moved out from Okahandja with three companies, two composed of veterans and one being a newly arrived marine infantry company. Four days later Estorff's force met and drove off a moderately large number of western Hereros at Otjihinamaparero. Though it was no more than a skirmish, the "battle" at Otjihinamaparero was blown up out of all proportion in the German press, which had been waiting nearly six weeks for the first German victory. Estorff's own dispatch made the fray sound vaguely like a second Sedan. "We fought for ten hours," he wrote, "against an enemy who was well entrenched among a field of large boulders. It was a hard grind for the sun burned hot and the thirst was almost unbearable, but by evening we had stormed their boulder fortress. I must say we fought a good fight and have won a richly deserved victory."[3] The Kaiser, who was following the progress of the

3. *Official History*, I, p. 78.

military operation with passionate interest and growing impatience, could not restrain his glee at the reports of a victory and immediately dispatched a message of congratulation couched in the high-flown language which characterized all of his official utterances: "On the occasion of your victorious fight of February 25 I send to Section Estorff my imperial good wishes and express my pleasure at the brave and steady behavior of my soldiers and marines. To the wounded I send my best wishes for a speedy recovery."[4] To the common soldier this worldwide attention was rather overwhelming. As one trooper noted in his daybook, "it is a fine feeling for a soldier to know that his All-Highest Warlord is thinking of him even when he is far away from home."[5]

To put the victory at Otjihinamaparero into some perspective, it should be recorded that the German official history claimed fifty enemy dead, while admitting that two Germans were killed in the action and seven were wounded. After the battle Estorff made contact with the garrison at Outjo, in accordance with his orders, and together they marched back toward Okahandja. Western Hereroland was thus secured by Estorff, but since the Hereros whom he had defeated were retreating in the general direction of the main force of their fellow tribesmen, the security of the west had been purchased at the price of forcing a concentration of the Herero tribes, something that Leutwin had specifically wished to avoid.

The East Section

The success of Estorff was in large measure due to the fact that two-thirds of his troops were veterans. Major Glasenapp, the commander of the East Section, was not so lucky: his force was made up entirely of new arrivals, two companies of marine infantry and two companies of replacement troops which were not yet completely organized when operations started. Despite the weakness of his force Glasenapp decided to exceed his orders, which called on him only to block the eastern frontier in

4. *Ibid.*, I, 79.   5. *Ibid.*

cooperation with the Gobabis garrison; he decided instead to seek out and destroy the Tjetjo Hereros who were known to be in the vicinity of Gobabis. Anxious to get on with the job, Glasenapp left Windhoek even before all his troops were ready to march—a decision that proved to be the first in a long series of errors. Herero guerrillas harassed his troops to such an extent that he was finally forced to make camp and wait for his full force to concentrate. Upon resuming the march, he learned that the Tjetjo Hereros had broken camp at Gobabis and were heading north. Sensing the opportunity for a great victory, Glasenapp turned to the north and began his pursuit of the enemy.

On February 25, 1904, Glasenapp and his column reached Kehoro only to find that the enemy had departed a few hours before. Despite the growing exhaustion of both horses and men, Glasenapp pushed on to Kanduwe, where he joined forces with the Gobabis garrison which was also pursuing the Tjetjos. Undeterred by the fierce heat and the shortage of water, Glasenapp ordered a patrol to reconnoiter as far north as the Eiseb River, in order to learn whether the enemy was positioned to the north. When the patrol returned four days later with the report that they had seen no trace of the Hereros, Glasenapp concluded that the enemy must have turned west in the hope of joining the Herero main force. Convinced that there was no longer any danger of the Hereros escaping into Bechuanaland, Glasenapp resolved to continue his pursuit to the west. At Okanjesu he picked up the scent again and drove his men relentlessly forward in the hope of catching the enemy before they joined up with Samuel Maharero. On March 12 Glasenapp's column reached Onjatu; both the horses and men desperately needed time to recover from the rigors of the preceding month, in which they had averaged no less than 20 miles a day, much of that distance through heavy country. Glasenapp reluctantly conceded that a period of recuperation was imperative for his men, but he himself was too impatient to give up when the quarry was so near. No sooner was camp established than he organized a patrol in force consisting of ten officers and 46 men.

Riding to the southwest, Glasenapp soon discovered evidence that the Hereros were no more than a few hours ahead of him. With growing excitement he pushed on, though it is not completely clear what he had planned to do should he have located the Hereros. Presently an aged Herero woman was found and upon interrogation she revealed that the Tjetjos were at that moment only a few miles away at a place called Owikokorero. After riding a few more minutes Glasenapp came upon a large herd of cattle which was guarded by a handful of Hereros. The herdsmen ran off at the approach of the Germans, and Glasenapp took possession of the herd. In the early afternoon Glasenapp's column emerged from the heavy brush in which they had been riding all day into a clearing about 1000 yards wide. As the horsemen were trotting across the open space, they came under heavy fire from a large force of Hereros hidden in the brush on the opposite side of the clearing.[6] The Germans, taking whatever cover they could find, formed a ragged line and began answering the fire from the bush. A machine gun was rushed forward to add firepower to the German line. The Hereros, who had a healthy respect for the Maxim gun, poured volley after volley into the men trying to set up the gun. So heavy was the fire that the machine gun never was brought to bear on the enemy. Glasenapp, sensing that he had led his men into a trap, ordered a retreat to the northeast where the supply wagons had been stationed. At the same time he dispatched an officer messenger to warn the main body at Onjatu. Once the wagon train was reached, the Germans were able to organize a rear guard which held off the Hereros long enough to permit the survivors of the patrol to make good their escape. In this battle, which lasted no more than thirty minutes, twenty-six Germans died. There are no reports of Herero losses, but they were probably insignificant. Glasenapp was so shaken by the battle that he ordered the East Section to build a semi-permanent camp at Onjatu where they could lick their wounds and await developments.

6. *Ibid.*, I, 66-71.

The Main Section

After Estorff and Glasenapp had left Windhoek for the bush in mid-February, Leutwein was left with only enough men to garrison the stations in central Hereroland and to guard the railroad. Therefore, until reinforcements arrived on March 1, 1904, he was obliged to remain inactive.[7] Even after the fresh troops began to arrive at Okahandja, most of his efforts were concentrated on problems of administration and organization, the one exception being that he sent a force of 230 men, commanded by Captain Puder, to drive the Hereros out of the lands south of the railroad. On March 2 Puder left Okahandja and two days later he fought his first action. As the German column was on the march to Klein Barmen, they came under fire from enemy troops entrenched in the hills that paralleled the German line of march. Puder ordered his men to take up positions several hundred yards to the south of the enemy trench line. After two hours of indiscriminate and probably ineffective fire, Puder ordered one company commanded by a Lieutenant Rosenberg to turn the enemy's left flank, the terminal point of which he designated as a large and easily identifiable tree. Rosenberg was rather taken aback. "In all honesty," he wrote later, "I must confess that my heart beat faster when I received this order for it called for me to cross a 150-meter-wide creek bed under heavy fire."[8] Obedient to the orders, Rosenberg led his men to a point opposite the tree which in Puder's opinion marked the furthermost extension of the enemy line, and there formed them up and gave the order to attack with fixed bayonets. The hundred men of the company scrambled down the bank into the creek bed and began the long handicap over the dry bed. Before they had gone more than a few yards, Rosenberg learned to his dismay that Puder had misjudged the length of the enemy line, and his men were caught in a crossfire. Though his situation was rather uncomfortable, Rosenberg pushed the attack home. The Herero commanders, fearing that their line might be pierced, ordered their men to break off the action and

7. *Ibid.*, I, 82-95.   8. *Ibid.*, I, 86.

retreat to the west. German losses were heavy and though a victory of sorts had been won, it was an open question what purpose such "victories" served.

On March 11 Leutwein gave orders for an attack on the Herero main force; the date set for the action was April 1, 1904. The order is of considerable interest, for it illustrates the difficulty in applying textbook solutions to problems that arise in colonial warfare. By the time he wrote the order, Leutwein had pieced together a reasonably accurate picture of the disposition of the Hereros. He knew that Samuel and the Okahandja Hereros were encamped to the north in the Onjati hills, and he estimated their strength at 1000 rifles; he also guessed correctly that the Tjetjo Hereros were moving westward for a rendezvous with Samuel; he thought the Omaruru Hereros after their defeat by Estorff were retreating to the east. This was only partly true, for though some of the Omaruru Hereros were moving in an easterly direction, others were moving to the south. Finally, Leutwein assumed that there were still 1000 Hereros south of the railroad. He planned to keep the Hereros to the south under observation while he caught Samuel's force and that of Tjetjo in a vise, his own men attacking from the west while Glasenapp attacked from the east. This plan was very much in accord with the tactical and strategic ideas current at the time, but it suffered from a fatal weakness: Leutwein failed to establish communication with Glasenapp, who remained in total ignorance of the part he was to play. Furthermore, Leutwein assumed that the Hereros would take part in no countermeasures and would oblige him by passively awaiting their destruction.

In late March Leutwein received two disconcerting pieces of news, the accuracy of which he could not evaluate. A lieutenant named Bayer told him that on March 28 Rosenberg reported from Osona to his superiors in Okahandja that a large number of Hereros together with their herds were crossing the Swakopmund riverbed and heading northeast. The garrison at Okahandja was called out. Franke, who was still ill, warned the officers who did not yet know anything about colonial warfare that a night battle with natives was extremely dangerous. The advice, as it turned out, was sound but not needed, for by the time the Okahandja garrison arrived at Osona the Hereros had already disappeared. One old woman was found and she told her captors that she was a member of the Otjimbingwe tribe, which had left their traditional homeland to the south of the railroad and was trekking into the Onjati hills to join Samuel. The concentration of Herero forces that Leutwein had hoped to avoid had become a reality; rather than facing 1500 rifles Leutwein now had to reckon with 2500. The news from Glasenapp suggested that Leutwein would be foolish to count on any substantial assistance from that quarter. The combination of unfavorable news and transportation delays induced Leutwein to put off the date for the opening of operations from April 1 to April 7, 1904. If it had not been for the constant pressure from Berlin, Leutwein might very well have delayed the attack for a much longer time, but his superiors would not hear of it.

On April 7, 1904, at four in the afternoon, a morose Leutwein led 800 German soldiers and 160 native auxiliaries out of Okahandja to do battle with the Hereros. The first day's march was uneventful, but on April 8, as the German column approached Mount Onganjira, a prominent peak which rises abruptly from the floor of the Otjisasu valley, they came under heavy fire. Following normal procedures Leutwein ordered his men to dismount and fan out. Even before the line was completely formed, the Hereros began an all-out attack on the German left flank with the intention of rolling up the line. This danger was only barely averted by the timely arrival of all the machine guns and artillery. In a desperate attempt to overcome German firepower by raw courage, the Herero warriors twice charged straight into the muzzles of the German guns. The courage of the men was sustained by the wild chanting of the women, who shrieked over and over again: "Who owns Hereroland? We own Hereroland!" In the end, however, the Maxims ruled the field, and the Hereros fell back leaving behind dozens of their dead comrades. Failing to turn the flank, Samuel broke off the engagement and slipped away from the Germans. So disgusted was he with what he considered the cowardly behavior of his troops that he personally executed six of his own men after the battle. German losses were fourteen dead and twelve wounded, while Herero losses were put at over 100 by the German official historians. The Germans took two prisoners; one died of wounds shortly after his capture, and the other was executed the next day for "trying to escape."[9]

Two days after the battle of Onganjira, Leutwein resumed the march to the northeast, in the general direction of the Herero retreat. The country was covered with a heavy growth of bush which provided excellent cover for Herero scouts, who silently watched and reported every move the Germans made to Samuel. Just before noon on April 10 the German column approached a waterhole at a place called Owiumbo. As the thirsty horses and men pushed eagerly forward toward the water, heavy enemy fire crackled out of the bush that surrounded the waterhole on three sides. Against an unseen enemy the German artillery and machine guns were largely useless. To have advanced into the bush would have been suicidal; to remain in the clearing was hardly an alternative. After several painful hours during which losses mounted and a sense of utter futility came over the men, Leutwein finally gave the order to retreat. The next day the Main Section straggled back into Okahandja defeated, and humiliated.[10]

Leutwein himself was badly shaken. "Public opinion in Germany," he wrote just after the defeat, "including many men with experience in Africa, has dramatically underestimated the Hereros. Even we in the colony had not expected such resistance. The Hereros apparently believe that they can expect no quarter and are therefore fanatically determined. They sacrifice themselves with equanimity. . . . The fighting will therefore come to an end only when the enemy has fired his last shot. The fight at Owiumbo proves that our troops at their present strength are not in fact capable of putting down the uprising. . . . In order to break their resistance our troops must be strong enough so that they will be able to attack the enemy all at once and not

9. Until the battle of Waterberg, German sources show that no prisoners at all were taken. See Drechsler, *Südwestafrika*, p. 178.
10. *Official History*, I, 103-111.

piecemeal as now. It is obvious that it is meaningless to talk of encirclement, for in order to encircle 50,000 people we would have to bring together more men than this water-poor and resourceless land could sustain."[11]

Despite his pessimism, which after the battle of Owiumbo bordered on despair, Leutwein was still under orders to seek out and destroy the enemy, and so he began to regroup his men for a second test. Before the regrouping was seriously begun, however, he received news of two more setbacks. First, he learned that Glasenapp's East Section had been ambushed a second time at Okaharui on April 3, 1904, with the loss of 32 men dead and 17 wounded. Then came news that typhus had broken out among the survivors of the East Section, and that the whole force had had to be quarantined. This meant that about one-quarter of the effective troops in South West Africa were for the moment completely out of action. In the last days of April 1200 officers and men arrived from Germany, but even with these reinforcements Leutwein showed no inclination to leave the safety of Okahandja for the dangers of the bush. In early May, Samuel Maharero broke camp and led his people one hundred miles to the north, where the pasture was better and the Germans further away. The withdrawal of Samuel ended the first phase of the Herero War and led to a long period of inactivity in which the Germans spent their time building up their supply base and training their men.

In four months the Hereros had made off with most of the cattle owned by whites and had destroyed virtually every farm in Hereroland. In six battles and a number of skirmishes they had defeated the Germans as often as they themselves had suffered defeat. In terms of losses it does not seem improbable that they had killed one German for every one of their own men that fell. By April the German troops were despondent, discouraged, and demoralized and their leaders were in despair. The greatest military machine in the world had ground to an inglorious halt, and it was unclear when and how it would be set in motion again.

11. *Ibid.*, I, 110-111.

The Hereros in Victory

Seen from the perspective of the Hereros, the March and April battles brought nothing but stunning victories. The reasons for their repeated successes are clear. In the first place, Samuel was operating from interior lines from a secure base in the Onjati mountains, while the Germans were forced to use the exterior lines with all the disadvantages inherent in that type of operation. Secondly, the Germans had serious problems with mobility, and these Samuel compounded by avoiding battle wherever he could and by forcing the Germans into long exhausting marches. As the weeks went by the Herero commanders became ever more adept at handling their men in battle, and they gradually developed a characteristic style of battle. Utilizing their knowledge of the country and ability to move easily through the bush, the Hereros tracked the Germans constantly. Every day messengers arrived at Samuel's camp, bringing him the latest information on the disposition of the German troops in the field as well as complete reports on the arrival of reinforcements. Armed with this knowledge, Samuel was able to set up ambushes at likely looking points along the German line of march. Once the battle was joined, the Hereros in almost all instances fought in the heavy bush, where the German firepower was of little value. None of the engagements was continued beyond the point at which losses became excessive. Though it is hard to establish the exact number of Hereros who were present at any given battle, it seems likely that their numbers were often much smaller than the German official historians believed.

A brief account of the battle of Okaharui will illustrate the tactical skill of the Hereros.[12] On April 1, 1904, Glasenapp was marching to the west under the impression that he was to join with Leutwin, who supposedly had left Okahandja on that day. In addition, he was under orders to prevent the escape of the Hereros in a northeasterly direction from their concentration in the Onjati hills. Glasenapp at first marched to the west; but upon learning that Leutwein had not left Okahandja and would

12. *Ibid.*, I, 111-119.

not depart for a week, and further learning that a large mass of Hereros was moving to the east, he doubled back and made for Onjatu. The line of march was two and one-half kilometers long. The Fourth Marine Company led the march, followed by the artillery, the company of colonial troops, twenty-two wagons filled with provisions, and the First Marine Company bringing up the rear. The men and beasts were exhausted by nearly a month of heavy marching, and morale was low. Their every move was apparently noted by Herero scouts. During the early morning of April 1, 1904, the Hereros began to close in on the rear guard; their presence was unnoticed by the Germans. At about 9:00 o'clock a small detachment of Hereros broke out of the bush and drew German fire. While distracted by this action, the German rear guard suddenly found itself attacked on three sides by an unseen enemy; within a few minutes the Hereros managed to split the rear guard, so that about one-half of the First Marine Company was completely cut off. Several times the Hereros advanced from the bush in an effort to overrun the German position, but each time they were driven back by concentrated fire. Seeing that it was futile to challenge the Germans in the open, the Hereros continued the fight from the heavy bush on both sides of the road. Glasenapp, who was with the van when the fight broke out, turned his column about and threw all his forces, artillery included, against the Hereros. About noon the Hereros broke off the engagement and disappeared. Pursuit was futile. The Germans lost 33 dead and 17 seriously wounded out of a force of 230. The Germans claimed to have counted 42 Herero bodies and believed that that number was perhaps less than half of the total Herero loss; they also believed that more than 1000 Hereros took part in the battle. Based on what one knows about official military historians and their accuracy, particularly in matters of enemy numbers and losses, one probably ought to be very skeptical about the figures.

More to the point, why did the Hereros use mass attacks rather than fighting from the bush? Two reasons are possible. In the first place, the Hereros were natural warriors and preferred to fight in the open where their courage could be seen by all. Given this disposition it was probably difficult for the leaders to hold back the warriors, particularly if they saw the enemy in disarray. Second, and more important, Glasenapp's column was well supplied with food and ammunition, and, even more tempting, it had artillery. It seems likely that the Herero leaders decided to stake everything on overwhelming the whole column in order to get their hands on the supplies and military equipment. In this they were defeated, but they were gambling for high stakes. Indeed, before the details of the battle were known, a rumor spread that the Hereros had in fact captured Glasenapp's cannons, and that rumor caused near consternation at German headquarters. The thought of fighting Hereros armed with cannons and machine guns was a prospect no German cared to contemplate.

Although we can only speculate on Samuel Maharero's precise objectives during these months, we do have an interesting account given by a German missionary of the spirit and morale of the Hereros during the weeks that they were in the Onjati hills. This missionary, named Kuhlmann, met Samuel and the Hereros at Otjosasu (a village about thirty miles to the east of Okahandja) on February 22 and stayed with them until March 6, 1904.[13] During that time the tribe moved to the south toward the Onjati hills. Kuhlmann believed that there were about 2000 warriors at Otjosasu, accompanied by about 4000 women, children, and herdsmen. He saw large numbers of cattle and wagons, and observed that most of the warriors had horses. Samuel, who was almost always surrounded by his captains, wore civilian clothes, but the warriors wore either their traditional costume—an ostrich-feather war-bonnet, a red kerchief, and a red waistband—or were outfitted in German uniforms. The general attitude of the Hereros was confident. Kuhlmann was impressed by the discipline. Orders were short but definite, and obeyed without delay. Scouts, some afoot and some riding, came and went continuously. Kuhlmann was taunted by the Hereros, who asked him to persuade Leutwein to leave Okahandja and fight in the open field. In a very interesting and revealing comment, the Hereros expressed their amazement that the Ger-

13. *Deutsche Kolonialblatt* (March 23, 1904), p. 208ff.

mans had repaired the railroad so quickly. They compared this activity to that of white ants who, no matter how many times their dwelling is destroyed, return to the work of rebuilding. The chief named Kajata bragged that some day all the Hereros —those at Otjimbingwe, Omaruru, Waterberg, and Gobabis— would unite and advance on Okahandja, where they would fight and die if they must, since that was their home and they would never give it up. Kuhlmann assumed that Kajata meant that the Hereros did not consider the skirmishes that had taken place so far as real fighting. Kuhlmann said that the most common complaint of the Hereros was the sharp dealing of the traders; one Herero told him that he should tell Leutwein to get rid of the traders, and that if this were done peace could be made. In general, most of the Hereros had nothing but praise for Leutwein and the government, which they believed dispensed even-handed justice to all. Kuhlmann also learned that among the common people there was some anxiety about a Herero victory, since they reasoned that if the leaders were successful they would expropriate the cattle of all the small herdsmen.

TABLE 2
Major Engagements and Estimated Losses

Date	Place	Herero losses	German losses
January 12-20	Opening battles	25 (?)	100
February 2	Omaruru	50	15
February 25	Otjihinamaperero	50	12
March 4	Klein Barmen	10 (?)	6
March 13	Owikokorero	10 (?)	30
April 9	Onganjira	100	20
April 13	Owiumbo	10 (?)	25
Total		250 (?)	210

SOURCE: Military Section, German General Staff, eds., *Die Kämpfe der deutschen Truppen in Südwestafrika* (2 vols., Berlin, 1907), vol. I.157. This source, cited in the text as *Official History*, lists all soldiers who were killed or who died during the entire course of the campaign. In addition to the name of the casualty, it also gives date of death, place of death, and probable cause. Herero losses are given in round numbers only.

At the end of April, Samuel was free to move about the land at will. Glasenapp and the East Section were for all purposes out of action at Owikokorero, and Leutwein was licking his wounds at Okahandja. Using this favorable opportunity, Samuel ordered his forces, which now included half or more of the entire Herero tribe, to break camp and head north for the Waterberg area. His reasons for this move were straightforward. First, such a mass of livestock had to be moved periodically or it would soon exhaust its fodder. Second, Samuel wanted to be as far away from the railroad as possible, for he knew that the effectiveness of the Germans was inversely proportional to the distance that they must operate away from their base of supplies.

1. Review of colonial troops, 1898.

2. German battery in action in Namaland.

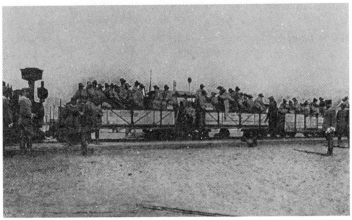

3. Reinforcements on the way from Swakopmund to Windhoek.

4. German soldiers drawing water.

5. Machine guns in action at Owiumbo.

6. German troops in camp.

7. General von Trotha and his staff at Waterberg.

8. Major Theodor Leutwein.

9. Leutwein and von Trotha (in uniform) at Windhoek,
   July, 1904.

10. German troops on the march in South West Africa(drawn from a soldier's sketch).

11. Herero "Pontoks."

12. Battlefield at Hartebeestmund.

13. Hendrik Witbooi.

14. Samuel Maharero.

15. Hendrik Witbooi.

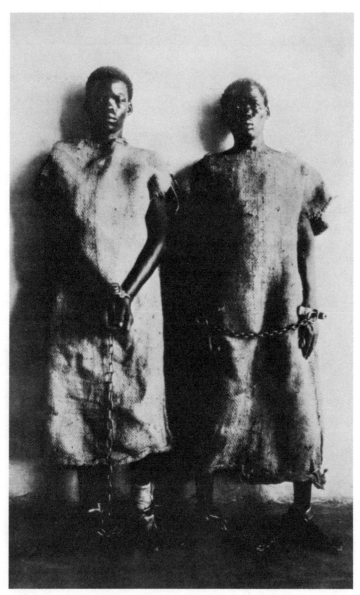
16. Herero prisoners in chains.

17. Morenga and his band.

18. Hereros returning from the Omahake Desert.

19. Hereros executed by the Germans.

5

The Battle
of Waterberg

AS THE REPORTS of one disaster after another poured
into Berlin during March and April 1904, a sense of frustration
came over the high command. The military hierarchy, which
up to that time had viewed the events in South West Africa with
a certain detachment, became passionately interested in ending
the war and their embarrassment as soon as possible. Their
new-found interest was goaded on by the emperor, who dressed
down his generals repeatedly for their failures. As a first step in
righting the boat, the general staff decided that Leutwein must
go. After his repeated defeats it was clear to everyone that he
lacked the ruthlessness, the military acumen, and the will necessary to bring the war to a rapid and successful conclusion. To
replace Leutwein the general staff selected General von Trotha,
a seasoned colonial fighter who had won a reputation for
ferocity in German East Africa a decade before. In entrusting
von Trotha with the task, the emperor was careful not to limit
his freedom of action by any specific instruction or directives.
"His Majesty the Emperor and King only said to me that he
expected that I would crush the uprising with any means necessary and then inform him of the reasons for the uprising";
thus von Trotha explained his commission to Leutwein.[1] "I
know the tribes of Africa," he continued. "They are all alike.

1. Drechsler, *Südwestafrika*, p. 180.

They only respond to force. It was and is my policy to use force
with terrorism and even brutality. I shall annihilate the revolting tribes with streams of blood and streams of gold. Only after
a complete uprooting will something emerge." From the defeats of the spring the government learned that colonial wars
demand lavish supplies of men and equipment. Accordingly
massive reinforcements were hastily prepared and dispatched to
South West Africa. Hamburg began to take on the aspects of a
wartime harbor. Between May 20 and June 17 five troop trans-
ports left, carrying 169 officers and administrators, 2185 men,
and 2000 horses.[2] Added to the more than 2000 men already in
South West Africa, this gave the Germans close to 5000 men to
deal with a tribe which Leutwein estimated had only 2500 rifles
and a limited supply of ammunition. The May and June reinforcements were only the first installment of a steady flow of
troops which would eventually reach almost 20,000 men.

On June 16, 1904, von Trotha arrived at Okahandja where he
held his first interview with Leutwein. Leutwein presented him
with a draft proclamation offering amnesty to the Hereros if
they would lay down their arms at once. "On the basis of my
experience I had come to the unalterable conviction that in the
vast, trackless wastes of South West Africa one could only defeat
the natives by utilizing the assistance of other natives," said
Leutwein. "If one did not offer the hand of reconciliation to the
rebels after they had had sufficient punishment one faced the
danger of unending conflict."[3] Von Trotha would have none of
it. "I said at once that in principle I was against such a means of
handling the uprising and that such a procedure ran completely counter to the intentions of His Majesty," he wrote of
Leutwein's proposal. Leutwein feared that von Trotha's methods would destroy one of the priceless assets of the colony,
namely its people, but he bowed to von Trotha's decision and
thereafter confined himself to his civilian administrative duties
which, since the military controlled all, were largely pro forma.

2. *Official History*, I, 130.
3. Drechsler, *Südwestafrika*, pp. 179-180.

The Preliminaries

During the two months from the time von Trotha arrived (June 13, 1904) until the day of the battle of Waterberg (August 11), the Germans made their intentions absolutely clear. Elaborate supply dumps were created; advance bases were set up; a whole communications network was established; and men and horses were brought forward to a line of stations that gradually surrounded the Herero positions at Waterberg. While all this activity was going on, numerous reconnaissance parties were sent into the area occupied by the Hereros.

Though we can speak with no certainty of the intentions of Samuel and his council of war, it does not seem unreasonable to suggest that he welcomed a battle precisely because he thought he could win it, or at least impose such losses on the Germans that they would give up and let him enjoy his spoils in peace. He was, of course, wrong, but not irrational. The battle of Waterberg was in fact closely contested. With a bit more luck the Hereros might well have defeated the Germans there, as they had done repeatedly in the opening days of the campaign. Though the German army was considerably larger at Waterberg than it had been four months before, and though the communications problems which had vexed Leutwein had been largely overcome, still these advantages were largely nullified by two other facts: the Germans were now operating three times as far away from their railroad as they had under Leutwein, and their soldiers were for the most part inexperienced in colonial warfare, whereas Leutwein had at least a core of highly experienced men.

From the time the Hereros withdrew from the Onjati hills to Waterberg until the arrival of von Trotha on June 13, 1904, military operations all but ended in South West Africa. The growing German army was too busy establishing bases, training the newly arrived troops, and creating a communications network to do more than watch the Hereros at a distance.

When von Trotha met with Leutwein on June 13 he learned that upward of 6000 Herero fighting men, together with perhaps 40,000 women and children, were encamped in the area to

TABLE 3
Departures from Hamburg, May-June 1904

May 20	Staff of Lieutenant General von Trotha; administrative staffs and base personnel. Total: 496 men, 73 officers, doctors, and officials; 420 horses.
June 1	First Company of the Second Regiment. Total: 13 officers, 192 men, 289 horses.
June 7	Second and Third Companies of the Second Regiment. Total: 19 officers, 341 men, 494 horses.
June 7	Seventh and Eighth Companies of the Second Field Regiment. One battery of artillery. Total: 26 officers, 485 men (this transport was destined for Lüderitz Bay).
June 17	Fourth, Fifth, and Sixth Companies of the Second Regiment. One Field Artillery battery. Total: 38 officers, 671 men, 923 horses.

the south of Waterberg. Despite the fact that the German forces in South West Africa were approaching parity with the enemy and their firepower was obviously much greater, von Trotha decided against quick action. A few days later he revealed his mind in his first dispatch to the General Staff in Berlin. "The Hereros are concentrated on the Omuramba," he wrote. "Samuel is at Okaitua and is said to be no longer eager to make war. Assa, who has more influence than any of the other chiefs, is apparently the driving force behind the party that wants to go on with the war. In the Paresis Hills there are still some small bands of Hereros and the Komas Hills still harbor a few robbers. In the Onjati Hills, however, where I have just conducted reconnaissance operations, there is no trace of the enemy. In other parts of Hereroland there are still some marauding bands, but the railroad has not been, up to this time, endangered."[4]

In von Trotha's view it was an open question whether the Hereros would fight or flee, but he made it plain to his supe-

4. *Official History,* I, 132.

riors in Berlin that he hoped they would not continue their trekking to the north or northwest, because if they did the Germans would have no way to follow them for months. To operate in the vicinity of Waterberg strained the German supply system to the utmost; had the Hereros put another 100 miles between themselves and the German railheads, von Trotha would have had no choice but to request funds to build a railroad to the north.

The most perplexing question of the Waterberg campaign, then, is why the Hereros failed to withdraw. There is no reason to think that the excellent reconnaissance system which had served Samuel so well when he was encamped in the Onjati Hills had broken down. Surely Samuel knew about the steady stream of German soldiers that were arriving by rail at Okahandja and from there being dispatched throughout Hereroland. Furthermore, Samuel could hardly have missed the fact that von Trotha was concentrating strong forces along a north-south line from Omaruru to Outjo, with the clear intention of blocking any retreat in that direction. By the middle of July one German company had advanced from Outjo to Naidous; two more companies had moved to Otjiwarongo; and Major Deimling with four companies of mounted infantry and six guns was on a rapid march to Ojambutu-Omusema-Uarei. Deimling was on the road that led to the gap between Little Waterberg and Mount Waterberg, and it was through that gap that the Hereros would have to pass if they intended to escape to the northwest. In the meantime, smaller units were on their way south from Otavi, while the main force under von Trotha himself was moving up from the south in three columns. From east to west these were as follows: Section von Estorff (four companies of mounted infantry, with four field pieces and four machine guns); Section von der Heyde (three companies of mounted infantry, with four field pieces and four howitzers); and Section Mueller (four companies of mounted infantry, with eight field pieces and six machine guns). By the first of July all these units were on the march. Samuel's response is highly suggestive. He made no move whatsoever to escape. He sent out no patrols to test which routes were still open but abandoned the Okason-

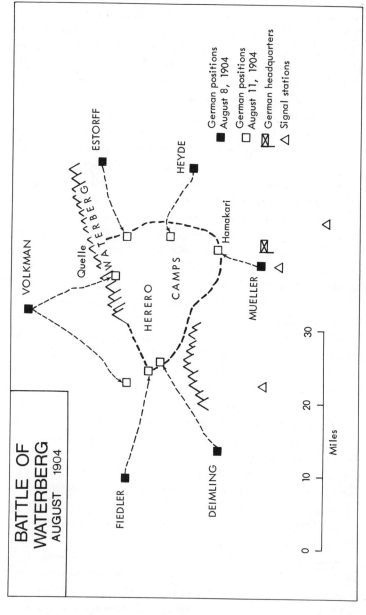

BATTLE OF
WATERBERG
AUGUST 1904

FIEDLER

VOLKMAN

Quelle

WATERBERG

ESTORFF

HERERO

CAMPS

HEYDE

Hamakari

DEIMLING

MUELLER

German positions
August 8, 1904

German positions
August 11, 1904

German headquarters

Signal stations

0   10   20   30
Miles

Map 7

goho-Okatua line and gathered his forces in an ever tighter circle. He ordered the construction of field fortifications, which consisted mainly of thorn bushes used like barbed wire. Undoubtedly, Samuel had every intention of meeting the Germans in a defensive battle, and one can only infer that he must have thought he could have defeated them; otherwise his failure to escape while the opportunity was still open is inexplicable.

Was Samuel's plan reasonable? He had at most 6000 able-bodied men against a German army that by August was approaching 5000 with three machine gun sections and 32 artillery pieces. Surely Samuel must have based his decision principally on the following factors. Whereas a steady stream of men was landing at Swakopmund, the number of men in the front line did not grow in proportion. On the eve of the battle, von Trotha was able to put into the field only about 1500 bayonets and thirty field pieces. Behind those troops were an ever-proliferating number of communication troops, hospital attendants, pay clerks, veterinarians, railroad troops, supply troops, transportation troops, horse drivers, stores officers, and reserves (three companies and one battery of them). Samuel was confident that the exhausting advance of one hundred miles or more would take a heavy toll of the German troops, sapping their strength and their morale.

How accurate this assumption was can be judged by a single incident. On June 22, 1904, von Trotha ordered Estorff to advance to the Omuramba-u-Omataka river course, which at that time marked the southern boundary of the Herero positions. From Okasondusu, where Estorff was encamped when he received the order, to the riverbed was about 25 miles. His troops got underway at seven in the morning, with the full expectation of reaching their destination by evening. The march was a punishing experience for both men and animals, and when at seven in the evening the goal was not yet in sight, Estorff ordered a halt in order to let the wagon carrying the reserve water catch up. After a rest of two and one-half hours, the march was resumed; at midnight Estorff, now unclear as to where he was, ordered a halt for the night. The next morning at first light the march was resumed, only to be stopped at midmorning as the heat and dust made further progress for the parched men and beasts all but impossible. Estorff sent out a number of patrols to locate water, but as the day ended each returned with the same message: no water to be found anywhere.

Estorff was in a desperate position: to stay where he was could only mean utter disaster for his 500 men, and yet he had no idea at all in which direction salvation lay. In desperation the Germans accepted the offer of a Herero prisoner they had picked up along the way; he promised to lead them to Karupuka, where he assured them they would find water. One of the old colonial hands disputed the man's story, saying that he had been to Karupuka in 1903 and seen that the waterholes there had all been dry. Estorff, however, had no other real alternative but to trust the fate of his force to an enemy prisoner. After burying the artillery and ammunition to lighten the loads on man and beast as much as possible, the section began a mad dash for safety. After four torturous hours, the straggling column entered the Omuramba-u-Omatako riverbed and less than an hour later they found their first water. It was muddy and brackish, but to the thirst-crazed animals and men it meant enough strength to push on. After drinking the vley dry, the column pushed on to Karupuka where, as the Herero prisoner had promised them, they found plentiful supplies of sweet water. The section was saved, and work parties were able to recover the buried guns and ammunition, but it was, as Wellington said, "a near run thing."

Samuel also counted on the thorns as a valuable ally. As one German report stated: "The worst enemy of the German soldiers, far worse than the Hereros themselves, is the thorn bushes which thickly cover the land. The Hereros are used to them, and indeed even take advantage of them, but they are for the white soldier just the same as hundreds of barbed wire entanglements and above all they preclude the effective use, on numerous occasions, of our artillery."[5] Given the conditions of the land and the relatively small German forces deployed against him, Samuel was apparently convinced that he had a reasonable chance of holding his own against the German army.

5. Bayer, *Mit Hauptquartier*, p. 57.

The flavor of the war in these months of waiting can be discerned from a few passages in a daybook kept by a Lieutenant Graf von Arnim, who commanded a patrol that probed deep into Hereroland in mid-June.[6] The patrol consisted of two officers, one NCO, nine enlisted men, four Witbooi scouts, and a civilian volunteer who knew the country. On the night of June 17 the patrol departed.

We rode through to the northwest through unbelievably thick bush. . . . Our goal was the Osandjache mountains which were to the west of the Little Waterberg. . . . At 6:00 P.M. just as the twilight hour began we reached a broad plain. Before us we saw the mountains which were our goal. Here we made an important observation. At the foot of the mountains dust clouds rose; therefore Okambukauandja was still in the hands of the enemy and he was not moving. The moon rose and the evening part of our journey began. After an hour ride the order came to halt. A fire was visible, apparently close in front of us. Melchier [the civilian], Khaynach [an NCO], and two Witboois went forward on foot. Presently they returned with the information that there was not one but two fires but they were a good distance off. Carefully we proceeded on. Again, "Halt!" Now we could smell smoke but could not see any fire. A man climbed a tree and discovered that there was a fire on our right. At the foot of the western slopes of Mount Waterberg he also reported several fires. It was clear therefore that we were in the midst of the area in which the Hereros were encamped. We had stumbled into the area unnoticed.

After spending an uncomfortable night surrounded by Herero camps, the patrol broke camp at 5:30 the next morning and pushed on, still unnoticed.

It gradually grew lighter and we again sent out flank patrols. A magnificent vista opened before us. Directly ahead lay the valley of the Omuweroumue, to the right the slope of the Little Waterberg, with cliffs 20 to 30 meters high which were of dark red stone in contrast to the green and brown slopes of the mountain. In front of us was the Great Mount Waterberg whose thickly wooded slopes were half lit by the rising sun in a marvelous array of colors and still half in darkness. To the left a small hill covered with cactus and reddish gold and green bushes interspersed among the cacti. Overhead a blue sky, directly in front

6. Paraphased from *Official History*, I, 137ff.

a clearing separated from us by some trees. There was some evidence of the enemy in the midst of this peace of God in nature, for there was smoke in the air and this smoke came from fires of the Hereros encamped along the base of the Little Waterberg and in the passes through the mountains. Our position was not very secure. If we were discovered and Samuel decided to cut off our retreat then we would have been in the soup. . . . We therefore thought it advisable to veer off to the left behind the hill with the cactus on it and from the top of this hill to orient ourselves a little more carefully. It was lucky that we did that. We crossed the main trail from Waterberg to Karibib undisturbed and hid ourselves. Salzmann, Melchior, and I clambered up the hill. We scarcely got to the top when we heard footsteps, laughter, and free and easy banter. We remained absolutely still, of that you can be sure. Right below the summit passed a troop of Hereros without any suspicion that the enemy was so close. Our luck held; we were unnoticed. Had we been discovered it would have been the end, for the Witboois who were holding our horses were too far away. The footsteps of the blacks disappeared through the bush and we had a quick look around. We saw not only the camps of the Hereros but also several dust clouds which indicated that cattle were being driven to pasture. There was no doubt that the enemy were permanently encamped here. Being careful to make no noise we returned to our comrades who had also heard Herero voices close by.

Because of the heavy underbrush we were able to push on to the north unseen. Our patrol on the left flank called me over and showed me a woman who was a little daffy and who had guilelessly crossed the clearing into our hands. As soon as she stepped into the bush she was seized by Melchior and Andries Witbooi. . . . The prisoner began to talk. She tried to lay a trap for us by suggesting that we let her go in return for the information that the cattle of Chief Zacharias were close at hand and only poorly guarded. We couldn't do her this favor. The one bird in hand was worth more to us than two in the bush. We set her on a horse and detailed a man to lead it. There she made a ridiculous figure, every fifth step she fell off. As she couldn't stay on the horse we had no alternative but to make her trot alongside the patrol. We had to keep her with us for as soon as feasible she had to be thoroughly questioned, even though we couldn't let her go until we ourselves were well on our way to safety. Hendrik and the other Witboois came to a tolerable understanding with the old woman and the interrogation was satisfactory. We learned the position of the enemy camps. . . . Concerning the morale of the fighting men the old woman could give no evidence. There were plenty of guns but a shortage of ammunition. There were many wounded from the battle of Onganjira. Food was short, pasture and water in ample supply. As with the ancient Germans the women went into battle with their men to embolden them. The wounded and the dead were carried off the field by the women. The majority of the tribe was encamped in the vicinity of the Little Waterberg. . . . We now knew enough. Our task was to get the information as fast as possible to the commanding officer. . . . About 10:00 in the morning we reached an opening about two kilometers across. Here we rested and the men took off their coats which they had worn in the night. Here too we ran into our first opposition. Lucky for us the devils fear ghosts at night and in the morning they sit huddled around their fires. Near an abandoned camp right on the edge of the clearing about 15 blacks appeared advancing toward us. . . . One chap stood upright and directed the others. We watched their maneuvers for a bit and then decided to ride on. To be sure the temptation was great to let the stalkers come nearer and then deal them a sudden blow, but we resisted it because if it came to fighting we would run the risk of being cut off. When we went into the bush we saw to the left some other blacks. Apparently they were there to entice us to approach them for they stood still. We, however, did not do them that favor. At six in the evening we were again at the waterhole where our horses drank the day before. For twenty-four hours they had had no water. Understandably they drank eagerly. . . . At 6:30 we went on. Unfortunately the Witboois got a little turned around and we did not get to Omurandu until 11:00. Whether we were north or south of our camp we could not determine at first so we made preparations to spend the night in the bush. Then we heard cattle. A reconnaissance showed that we were only about 500 meters from the camp. We got back just in time, for the soldiers there planned to break camp the next morning. Everyone congratulated us on our patrol. We had been in the very midst of the Herero camp.

The Battle

Von Trotha continued to draw up his forces. By July the German army in South West Africa included 25 companies of mounted troops, 36 artillery pieces, and 14 machine guns. In addition, there was a large array of support troops which continually grew. By the end of July, 4000 men and 10,000 horses and oxen were deployed in a great circle around Waterberg. On

August 4, von Trotha issued his order for the coming battle. Its key sentence read: "I want to attack the enemy . . . simultaneously with all sections in order to annihilate him."[7] In the iron ring which von Trotha had forged around the Hereros there was a single weak link; the southeastern quadrant was only lightly held. Leutwein noticed this weak point and suggested to von Trotha that it be strengthened, but the general refused to modify his plans. The only possible explanation is that von Trotha, realizing that he did not have enough men to complete the work of destroying the Hereros, decided to let them escape to the southeast where they had no place to go but the Omaheke desert.

On the evening before the battle a small German detachment scaled Mount Waterberg, where they had a view of the whole country to the south.[8] Here they established a signal station which permitted von Trotha to keep in close contact with his various units during the battle. The Hereros, recognizing the importance of the station, tried desperately to dislodge the Germans but failed. As a result the Germans on the mountain had a bird's-eye view of the whole battle of Waterberg.

Before dawn on August 11, 1904, the six sections moved out. The largest, Section Deimling, was to attack the Hereros from the west along the base of Mount Waterberg. The third battalion, commanded by Lieutenant Colonel von Mueller of the first regiment, was ordered to attack from the south. (The commander of the third battalion, von Mühlenfels, was injured the night before the battle and was replaced by the regimental commander von Mueller.) Major Estorff, commanding the first battalion of the first regiment, was to lead the attack from the east. To the north two smaller sections were stationed to block the passes through the Waterberg hill mass to prevent any escape in that direction. Finally, the second battalion of the first regiment, commanded by von der Heyde, was to attack from the southeast.

Four of the six sections met little or no opposition. Von Estorff pushed to within a few miles of the town of Waterberg,

7. *Ibid.*, I, 152-155.   8. *Ibid.*, I, 158.

TABLE 4
Organization of German Forces
at the Battle of Waterburg

Commander in Chief: Lieutenant General von Trotha

A. Mounted Troops

1. First Field Regiment (Lieutenant Colonel Mueller)

III Battalion	II Battalion	I Battalion
(Major von Mühlenfels)	(Major von der Heyde)	(Major von Estorff)
Companies:	Companies:	Companies:
11th, 10th, 9th, 8th	7th, 6th, 5th, 4th	3rd, 2nd, 1st

2. 2nd Field Regiment (Colonel Deimling)

III Battalion	II Battalion	I Battalion
(Major von Lengerke)	(Major Meister)	(Major von Wahlen)
Companies:	Companies:	Companies:
9th, 8th, 7th	6th, 5th, 4th	3rd, 2nd, 1st

B. Field Artillery

II Section	I Section
Batteries:	Batteries:
8th, 7th, 6th, 5th	4th, 3rd, 2nd, 1st

C. Machine Gun Detachment

2nd Machine Gun Section	Marine Machine Gun Section	1st Machine Gun Section

D. Communication troops

Telegraph Section   Signal Section

E. Native Troops

Bethanier	Basters	Witboois

F. Train

Baking Column   Field Hospitals (9)

G. Support Areas

Railroad Detachment	Transport Troops	Sanitary Section
Artillery Depots	Horse Depots	Clothing and
Provision Office		Arms Depots

H. Replacement Troops

3rd Replacement Company	2nd Replacement Company 1st Replacement Battery	1st Replacement Company

meeting one small Herero force but otherwise without opposition. His total losses for the day were only one killed and twelve wounded. Deimling, with the largest force, took Waterberg, meeting only nominal opposition and suffering no losses. The two smaller forces in the passes also met no opposition, as no Hereros attempted to escape to the north. The only serious fighting was to the south and the southeast. Section Mueller broke camp at 2:30 on the morning of August 11 and just after daybreak reached the Hamakari riverbed. Here a lively firefight developed which lasted most of the day. The Germans were outnumbered and outfought, and in the late afternoon Section Mueller was surrounded and begging for assistance by heliograph. In the end, however, German fire-power prevailed and the Hereros fell back. German losses were 12 dead and 33 wounded. Section Heyde also received considerable punishment during the day but managed to hold its ground against superior enemy forces. When night fell the Hereros, despite the fact that they had inflicted heavy losses on both Sections Mueller and Heyde, were in desperate straits. Not only were there strong enemy forces in their rear, but German artillery was taking a terrible toll of the densely packed rear area where more than 50,000 men, women, and children and perhaps as many cattle were compressed into a rectangle only 5 miles wide and 10 miles long. Samuel and his chiefs decided that further resistance was futile and therefore gave orders to break out at any cost. The panic-stricken Herero masses followed the path of least resistance, which was to the southeast. Upon hearing that the Hereros had abandoned the struggle von Trotha ordered his troops to break contact with the enemy. No attempt was made to stop the escaping Hereros nor were they harassed. Von Trotha merely insured that the mass of Hereros did not move to the north or the south. As long as they moved in an easterly direction toward the desert they were unmolested.

The appearance of the Herero camps gave a clear indication of the extent of the defeat they had suffered. "The scene which unfolded will be forever in my memory," wrote one observer. "For several kilometers along the Hamakari there were camps which had a short time before provided shelter for many thousands of men and cattle. Whatever was within range of our guns had been destroyed and everywhere there were signs of wild panicky flight. In the lean-tos cowered old men and women and children who had been left behind. The wounded, sick, and dying awaited their fate crouched in corners. Everywhere there were numerous cattle left behind in their haste—and cattle are sacred to the Hereros—as evidence of the hysterical flight. Wagons filled with goods, furs, household items, apparently readied for flight, had been left behind. Numerous blankets, jewelry, whole cases of feathers were strewn about . . . the whole national wealth of the Hereros lay on those roads. . . . The general [von Trotha] forbade the killing of women and children but all armed men who were captured soon met their fate. A fearful punishment rained down upon the Hereros; they will never recover from it."[9]

The Pursuit

Von Trotha reported to his government as follows: "The battle was fought under conditions for which our troops were little prepared, that is to say: thick underbrush, an enemy who knew the ground exactly and was master at concealing himself, who was superior in numbers, who was free from logistic problems and even for caring for the wounded—all of which created the constant problem of his outflanking us and setting up a crossfire. Such a battle with such an enemy placed heavy demands on the physical and moral capacities of our officers and men. From my own observation as well as from the reports I received

9. *Ibid.*, 185-186.

I can say that the behavior of our brave troops was splendid. They displayed a steady discipline which never failed even in the most difficult situations. That officer losses, despite the fact that officers wore the same uniforms as the men and were similarly equipped, were relatively high gives evidence of their valor in battle."[10]

The Kaiser answered: "With thanks to God and with great joy I have received your report from Hamakari concerning the successful attack of August 11 against the main force of the Hereros. Though the heavy losses suffered because of the stiff resistance of the enemy are to be regretted yet the bravery which the troops displayed under the greatest tension and deprivation . . . fill me with pride, and may I give to you, to your officers and men my imperial thanks and fullest recognition of what you have done. William."[11]

This exchange of pleasantries concealed the fact that the German troops, despite von Trotha's orders, went on an orgy of bloodletting when they broke into the Herero camps, killing men, women, and children indiscriminately. One Hendrik Campbell, who commanded a unit of the native troops, said under oath: "When the fight was over, we discovered eight or nine sick Herero women who had been left behind. Some of them were blind. They had water and food. The German soldiers burned them alive in the huts in which they lay."[12] Shortly thereafter Campbell turned 70 Herero prisoners over to the Germans. Two days later he found that they had all been killed. A Berg Damara leader who had fought with the Germans also testifying under oath said that "We hesitated to kill Herero women and children, but the Germans spared no one. They killed thousands and thousands. I saw this slaughter for day after day." When word of the slaughter filtered back to Germany, the Chancellor, von Bülow, was angered and demanded an explanation from the chief of the General Staff, von Schlieffen. Schlieffen's explanation repeated the official military line, that the fighting had turned into a race war and the men were not responsible for their actions. "If it has happened that occa-

10. *Ibid.*, I, 190.   11. *Ibid.*, I, 191.
12. Drechsler, *Südwestafrika*, p. 186.

sionally women were killed, still it should be borne in mind that women not only took part in the fighting, but were the principal instigators of the cruel and awful tortures which were so often inflicted on our wounded men and that the soldiers were driven to an uncontrollable rage by the sight of the victims whose bodies were displayed with bestial premeditation."[13] Though Schlieffen's account was not really very convincing, the chancellor was not interested in pursuing the matter further.

The battle of Waterberg did not end the Herero War. The Hereros were demoralized but not yet impotent. Throughout Hereroland small bands continued to make periodic raids on German cattle while the mass of the people moved slowly but inexorably toward the Omaheke. On August 30 the Germans had established a series of heavily armed camps along the edge of the desert: Deimling at Epikuro and Kalfontein, Heydebreck at Klein Okahandja, Estorff at Okatawbaka, and Mühlenfels at Otjinene. Far out into the desert wastes, the Hereros were frantically searching for water. German patrols later found holes as deep as forty feet dug by Hereros in a desperate attempt to find water. On September 28 a small band of Hereros tried to break through the German lines; they were repulsed almost without a fight. "All contacts with the enemy since the battle of Waterberg have demonstrated [that] strength of will, unity of command, and the last remnants of resistance have been lost,"[14] wrote von Trotha. The trails through the desert were littered with hundreds of carcasses. Prisoners reported that the people were weary of the war and willing to surrender. They also told that Samuel and several other leaders had crossed the desert and found refuge in British territory.

On October 2, 1904, von Trotha promulgated his famous "Schrecklichkeit" order in an attempt to stamp out the last embers of the revolt before the end of the year. The order read as follows:

Osombo-Windimbe October 2, 1904

I, the great general of the German troops, send this letter to the Herero People. Hereros are no longer German subjects. They have murdered, stolen, they have cut off the noses, ears, and

13. *Ibid.*   14. *Official History*, I, 206.

other bodily parts of wounded soldiers and now, because of cowardice, they will fight no more. I say to the people: anyone who delivers one of the Herero captains to my station as a prisoner will receive 1000 marks. He who brings in Samuel Maharero will receive 5000 marks. All the Hereros must leave the land. If the people do not do this, then I will force them to do it with the great guns. Any Herero found within the German borders with or without a gun, with or without cattle, will be shot. I shall no longer receive any women or children; I will drive them back to their people or I will shoot them. This is my decision for the Herero people.

The Great General of the Mighty Kaiser

This order is to be read to the troops at quarters with the additional statement that even if a trooper captures a captain of the Hereros he will receive the reward, and the shooting of women and children is to be understood to mean that one can shoot over them to force them to run faster. I definitely mean that this order will be carried out and that no male prisoners will be taken, but it should not degenerate into killing women and children. This will be accomplished if one shoots over their heads a couple of times. The soldiers will remain conscious of the good reputation of German soldiers.[15]

Two days later von Trotha explained his order to Schlieffen.

There is only one question for me: how to end the war? The ideas of the governor and the other old African hands and my ideas are diametrically opposed. For a long time they have wanted to negotiate and have insisted that the Hereros are a necessary raw material for the future of the land. I totally oppose this view. I believe that the nation as such must be annihilated or if this is not possible from a military standpoint then they must be driven from the land. It is possible by occupying the waterholes from Grootfontein to Gobabis and by vigorous patrol activity to stop those trying to move to the west and gradually wipe them out. . . . My knowledge of many central African peoples, Bantu and others, convinces me that the Negro will never submit to a treaty but only to naked force. Yesterday before my departure I ordered the execution of those prisoners captured and condemned in the last few days and I have also driven all the women and children back to the desert to carry the news of my proclamation. . . . The receiving of women and children is a definite danger for our troops, to take care of them

15. Drechsler, *Südwestafrika*, p. 184.

is an impossibility. . . . This uprising is and remains the beginning of a racial war.[16]

The immediate impact of von Trotha's decision to annihilate the Hereros was unfavorable. Leutwein, who was still governor, cabled the Foreign Office: "According to reliable reports the Hereros have asked for terms. Up to now the question of negotiation has been decided without consulting me. Therefore I ask for clarification: how far does my authority extend?"[17] When the Foreign Office answered that von Trotha alone had authority to deal with the natives, Leutwein asked to be relieved of his duties. Nor was Leutwein the only German disturbed by von Trotha's *modus operandi*. The highest civilian in the colony after the dismissal of Leutwein, Regierungsrat Tecklenburg, said that in his opinion German prestige with the natives was "lost beyond recall" by the actions of von Trotha. Even the government was alarmed by the bad press that the military action in South West Africa was receiving. On November 23, 1904, the Chief of the General Staff, Count von Schlieffen, informed Bülow of the army's position.

According to all appearances our troops will be forced to stop the enemy from returning to the west by a system of extended posts and will have to carry on a war of attrition with all its horrors such as typhus, malaria, and heart attacks. . . . It is conceivable that in such circumstances the call for a quick peace will be raised. With rebels, however, a peace can only be concluded on the basis of unconditional surrender. Up to now neither the whole Herero nation nor even part of it is amenable to such conditions. Prisoners whom Major von Estorff had captured were released after good treatment in order to win their fellow countrymen over to the idea of accepting German protection, but they have not been seen since. If the Hereros will not come in freely then they must be forced and encouraged to give up. To enter into negotiations with the Herero captains for this purpose is out of the question. They have forfeited their lives and in order to create acceptable conditions in the protectorate, they must be removed from office. If General von Trotha has put a price on the heads of the captains, then he has adopted the customary way of getting rid of them. The sums which he

16. *Ibid.*, p. 189.   17. *Ibid.*, p. 191.

offered are, however, clearly too low and must be expressed not in terms of money but rather in terms of head of cattle. When the influence of the captains is broken, then one can hope for the surrender of Hereros in meaningful numbers.

The measures which von Trotha has taken according to the two appendices (von Trotha's report of October 4 and the order of October 2) are prejudicial to such an outcome. One can agree with his plan of annihilating the whole people or driving them from the land. The possibility of whites living peacefully together with blacks after what has happened is very slight unless at first the blacks are reduced to forced labor, that is, a sort of slavery. An enflamed racial war can be ended only through the annihilation or complete subjugation of one of the parties. The latter course is, however, not feasible considering the present estimate of the length of the struggle. The intention of General von Trotha can therefore be approved. The only problem is that he does not have the power to carry it out. He must remain on the western edge of the Omaheke and cannot force the Hereros to leave it. If they should voluntarily leave the land we would not have gained much. They would present a constant threat in Bechuanaland in the event that the Cape Government would not or could not render them harmless.

There is therefore scarcely any other alternative but to try to persuade the Hereros to give up. That is made more difficult by the proclamation of General von Trotha which states that any Herero who tries to give up will be shot. If a new proclamation is issued which states that any Herero who gives up will be spared, they will scarcely trust this statement. Yet it must be tried. I believe therefore that it must be proposed to General von Trotha that (1) a higher price be put on the heads of the captains and the leaders; (2) by means of a new proclamation or in some other suitable way we spare the lives of those Hereros who give themselves up.[18]

Put in another way, Schlieffen did not suggest that he was offended by von Trotha's way of making war, but he was convinced that it would not be successful. On the strength of this letter, Bülow asked the Kaiser to lift the "Schrecklichkeit" order. He gave four reasons for doing so: (1) a policy of total annihilation was un-Christian; (2) it was not feasible; (3) it was economically senseless; and (4) such a way of making war would give Germans a bad reputation among civilized people. The Kaiser, even when pressured by his Chancellor and Chief

18. *Ibid.*, pp. 192-194.

of General Staff, was reluctant to order von Trotha to lift the order. For over three weeks he delayed, despite pressure from Bülow, until finally in late December he gave in. Von Trotha was equally reluctant, and when he finally bowed to the inevitable he did it with as bad a grace as possible. Those Hereros who surrendered would not be shot, that much he conceded, but they were to be chained, used for forced labor, branded with the letters GH (*gefangene Herero*), and any who refused to reveal the whereabouts of weapons caches were to be shot out of hand.

When the new policy went into effect in the beginning of 1905 the Herero revolt, or what was left of it, quickly flickered out. The surviving Hereros either voluntarily presented themselves at collecting stations or were driven there by German patrols. Between 50,000 and 60,000 Hereros had survived the battle of Waterberg and went to the Omaheke. Of those, about 1000 reached British territory; rather less than 1000 found refuge in Ovamboland; and perhaps the same number escaped to Namaland. An undetermined number filtered back through the German lines to their old homeland where they scratched out a living stealing cattle. In September 1905, a sweep was made through Hereroland which netted 260 prisoners and 86 guns. During this operation about 1000 Hereros were killed. After September there could hardly have been more than a few dozen free Hereros in all of Hereroland. In the German camps there were 10,632 women and children and 4137 men. To this number must be added the 4000 to 5000 Hereros in Bechuanaland, Namaland and Ovamboland. One year before, the Herero tribe had numbered close to 80,000 souls; in the summer of 1905 no more than 20,000 of those were still alive. So demoralized were the survivors that it did not seem possible that the tribe as such would ever recover from the catastrophe.

"The death-rattle of the dying and the shrieks of the mad . . . they echo in the sublime stillness of infinity!"[19] So one German soldier described the end of the Hereros. The German official historians were blunter: "The Hereros ceased to exist as a tribe."[20]

19. *Official History*, I, 214.   20. *Ibid.*

6

The Hottentot Revolt

IN THE AUTUMN of 1904, as the Hereros were expiring by the thousands on the Omahake wastes, the Hottentots, who up to that time had remained loyal to their German overlords, rose in a general revolt. Just why the Hottentots, who in January had spurned Samuel Maharero's plea for a simultaneous uprising, should have selected this unfavorable moment to cast the die is not altogether clear, but such evidence as we have suggests that their action was not as irrational as it appears at first glance. The key to understanding the Hottentots was, of course, the legendary Hendrik Witbooi.[1] Had the old chief remained true to his long-standing alliance with the Germans, his prestige alone would probably have been sufficient to guarantee peace in the south, but once he raised the standard of revolt he was able to carry most of the tribes of the south with him.

Before the German protectorate was established, Hendrik had fought long and bitter wars with the Hereros. Though he had failed to gain his ultimate objective, the establishment of Hottentot hegemony over the whole of the central plateau, still he had won a reputation as the most formidable captain north of the Orange River. In the 1890's he had challenged the Germans, and though in the end he was defeated, yet it was a defeat with honor. The Germans had such respect for his military prowess that they offered to make him an ally. Hendrik accepted their

1. Hendrik Witbooi deserves a full-scale biography, but as of yet none exists.

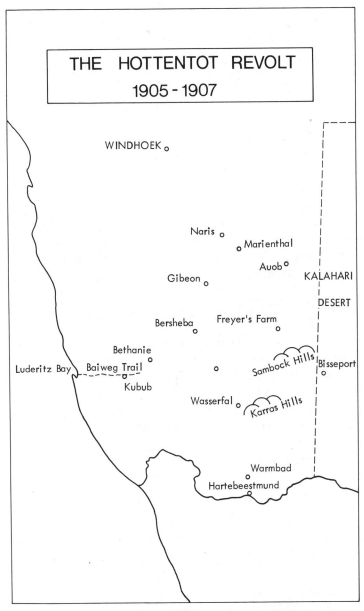

THE HOTTENTOT REVOLT
1905 - 1907

WINDHOEK

Naris
Marienthal
Auob
KALAHARI
Gibeon
DESERT
Bersheba
Freyer's Farm
Bethanie
Luderitz Bay Baiweg Trail
Sambock Hills Bisseport
Kubub
Wasserfal
Karras Hills
Warmbad
Hartebeestmund

Map 8

offer and on six occasions from 1896 to 1904 he came to the assistance of his colonial masters in putting down local disturbances. To the Germans Hendrik was diffident but unawed. When Leutwein tried to impress upon him the limitless power of imperial Germany, Hendrik replied simply: "I know very well that the German Emperor is more powerful than I, but you do not need to keep telling me about it." According to Leutwein, who knew Hendrik well, his dominating characteristic was his inclination toward mysticism. Even as a young man Hendrik was a devoted Christian, and as he grew older he grew more and more fanatically Christian. He frowned upon alcohol, took vigorous measures against Sabbath breakers, and like many Christians, he believed that the ultimate sin was sexual immorality. When his daughter killed an illegitimate child she had borne, because she feared his wrath, he ordered her put to death. Only the intervention of local German authorities prevented him from carrying out his awful judgment.

The Origins of the Hottentot Revolt

In the spring of 1904 Hendrik fell under the influence of a self-styled prophet named Stürmann, who had only recently arrived in South West Africa from the Cape. Stürmann proclaimed that he had been sent by God to drive the white man from Africa. His battle cry was "Africa for the Africans." That Stürmann exercised a powerful influence over Hendrik Witbooi is clear from a letter the old chief wrote to several other Hottentot captains explaining his decision to take the field against the Germans.

Rietmond 1. 10. 04

To my sons and brothers and captains Christian Goliath at Berseba and Paul Fredericks at Bethanie:
    Because I have little paper I write to my dear friends a single letter which our noble Christian must read and then send quickly on to Paul. My sons, as we all know for a long time I have lived under the law, and in the law, just as we all have in the hope that God the Father would determine the time to free us from the difficulties of this world. For I have borne everything with peace and patience and I have endured everything that

oppressed my heart because I waited for the Lord. Now I will not waste many words. Therefore I will speak about two points in the hope that you will understand me. First my arm and shoulder are lame and I recognized that the time is now full for God the Father to free the earth. So I give this letter for my dear ones to read as quickly as possible and then send the letter on to Paul. The second point is: I have now stopped walking submissively and will write a letter to the Captain [von Burgsdorff] saying that I have put on the white feather [the sign for commencing hostilities] and that the time is over when I will walk behind him. The time has expired and the Saviour himself will now act and he will free us through his grace and compassion. . . .[2]

The references to God the Father being about to free the earth apparently stem from Stürmann's teaching, but it would be wrong to imagine that Hendrik raised the standard of revolt in a fog of religious mysticism. More important in making his decision was his reading of the attitude of the Germans, both the military leaders and the settlers. Hendrik was disturbed by the fact that Leutwein, whom he trusted, had been pushed aside by von Trotha, a man who made no secret of his belief that the security of the colony demanded the disarming of all natives, friend and enemy alike. Rumors were rife during the middle of 1904 that the Germans were about to take some type of action against their native allies. The arrival of 300 German troops in Namaland in April gave some substance to these rumors. The anxieties of the Hottentots were not calmed by the attitude of the settlers, who made no secret of their hatred of all the "Kaffirs." In the pages of the settlers' newspaper, the *Deutsch-Südwest-Afrikanische Zeitung*, any black man who could read German could see what was in store for the natives if the settlers had their way. Captain von François was quoted by the newspaper as declaring that "the battle axes should not be buried until *all the tribes* have been disarmed [emphasis added]."[3] And his statement accurately reflected the sentiments of the settlers as a group. When Hottentot leaders asked German officials about the published threats, they received evasive answers which

2. See Leutwein, *Elf Jahre*, p. 457.
3. Drechsler, *Südwestafrika*, p. 200.

gave rise to the suspicion that the government officials had adopted the view of the settlers. Leutwein was sufficiently alarmed by the settlers' talk of vengeance even against the loyal tribes in the south that he tried to force the editor of the paper to show some moderation, but his efforts were of no avail. Despite Leutwein's fears that public discussion of postwar policy toward the Hottentots was unwise, in private his views were not much different from those of the settlers. On June 5, 1904, in a letter to the Colonial Department in Berlin, he recommended that at a "suitable time" the Hottentots should be disarmed and reduced to the level of a subject people. He added that he "welcomed" the uprising, for it gave the government an opportunity to make a new departure in the question of native relations.[4]

Suspicion about German intentions was, however, only part of the reason for Hendrik Witbooi's decision to forsake the German alliance. Combined with his growing suspicion that once the Herero war was won, the Hottentots would be next, was a streak of contempt for the vaunted military prowess of the Germans. During the fiascos of 1904, a German official reported that "many natives in the south have doubts about whether the power of the Germans is really as great as had been believed up to that time."[5] Even the German "victory" at Waterberg was, in the view of Hendrik, ambiguous. True, the Hereros had been defeated, but the Germans with all their men and equipment could not prevent the escape of the beaten foe.

In September 1904 the unrest in Namaland received new impetus when nineteen Hottentot scouts returned to their homes after having fled from the Germans. When Hendrik first heard that some of his men had deserted, he hastened to assure Leutwein that he himself remained loyal, and he blamed the incident on "false stories" that were circulating. He added that he was certain that the remaining Hottentot auxiliaries would remain true to their colors. The actual arrival of the deserters, however, put a different complexion on the matter. They deserted, they said, because the Germans had ill-treated them, and

4. *Ibid.*   5. *Official History*, II, 2.

were slaughtering the natives in the north without pity. Hendrik was both angry and hurt. He had been used to being treated as an honored ally by the Germans; he had been decorated by the German Kaiser; he considered the German officials to be his personal friends. Now he learned that his men were treated not as allies, but as slaves.

By the beginning of October the air was full of rumors that Hendrik was about to move against the Germans, and Leutwein wrote to ask him point-blank what his intentions were. Instead of answering, Hendrik ordered a general attack on the Germans in Namaland.

Morenga

Several weeks before Hendrik began hostilities in the south, fighting had already erupted there between a "robber baron" named Morenga and the Germans. Where Morenga came from, what his motives were, and why he decided to attack at that moment are not completely clear. Of his parents we know only that his father was a Hottentot and his mother a Herero. He received some education at a mission school and according to one report spent six months in Europe. He spoke with varying proficiency at least five languages, including Dutch, English, German, and several native languages. At the turn of the century Morenga was working in a copper mine in the Cape Colony. About 1903 he returned to South West Africa and took part in the Bondelzwarts rebellion. The Germans considered him one of the leaders of that revolt and sentenced him to death in absentia. Both as a military leader and as a man Morenga made a powerful impression on the Germans. Their accounts of him emphasized over and over again his Grossmut (magnanimity), his Umsicht (prudence) and his Tatkraft (energy)—three character traits which, in the European view, were conspicuously lacking in most natives. Germans explained Morenga's "whiteness" by noting that he had spent long years at the Cape and "had been accustomed to a certain degree of higher culture." As befitted a cultured man, Morenga carried on civilized warfare. His men never looted, but instead presented their victims with a precisely itemized requisition that guaranteed the recipient a period of immunity before a second requisition would be presented. Furthermore, Morenga did not allow the men to kill women, children, or even the wounded. He treated his prisoners in a courtly manner and often followed the eighteenth-century tradition of paroling them. Even when the Germans violated a truce, as they did twice, he took no revenge on their negotiators, who were both times in his power.

In June 1904 Morenga with about 30 men crossed the border at Bisseport and began his career as a robber. A few days later he established a fortified camp in the Sambock hills and made a series of raids on the nearby farms. Stories of his audacity brought a stream of recruits to his band. In August the Germans dispatched a Lieutenant named Stempel and 32 men to locate Morenga and prevent him from recrossing back into British territory with his loot. On August 29 Stempel was ambushed at a farm owned by a Boer named Freyer. In a short but deadly fire-fight Stempel and three of his men were killed and four others wounded. The sequel to the fight at Freyer's farm (which was omitted from the official history) is revealing of the German manner of making war. Suspecting that Freyer, who was a white man, and his sons, who were half-castes, "favored the rebels," the Germans convened a drumhead court-martial and sentenced the sons to death. A firing squad carried out the order the same day. Freyer, on the other hand, was remanded to a civilian court at Keetsmanhoop.

After the fight at Freyer's farm, Morengo shifted his base of operations to the Karras hills. In this rugged area he disappeared without a trace for several weeks only to reappear on October 5 at a place called Wasserfal, where the Eighth Field Company was bivouacked. Striking before dawn, Morenga and his men liberated all the company's horses and got away before the half-dressed troopers could stop them.

The Outbreak of the Hottentot Revolt

Though Morenga had broken the tenuous calm that had settled over Namaland after the peace of Kalkfontein, his influence was confined to individual natives, and did not spread to tribes. Only Hendrik Witbooi had sufficient prestige to stir up a full-scale war in the south. On October 3, 1904, two Witboois told the highest German official in Namaland, Bezirksamtmann von Burgsdorff, that Hendrik was about to go on the warpath. Burgsdorff, who knew Hendrik well and believed that he had considerable influence over the old chief, rode at once to Hendrik's camp at Marienthal, hoping to dissuade him from breaking the peace. As Burgsdorff entered the Hottentot camp he was shot down by a Baster-Hottentot named Salomon Sahl. The editors of the German official history sentimentalized the death of Burgsdorff (who was admittedly a decent, hard-working official) and said that he had been killed by members of a tribe "for whom he had done only good in the preceding ten years."[6] The Germans obviously believed that Hendrik had lured Burgsdorff to his camp to kill him, but there is little evidence to support that opinion. In all likelihood Sahl's action was his own doing and did not reflect the wishes of Hendrik. At any rate, Burgsdorff's murder was the signal for a general uprising. In the next few days about 40 German soldiers and civilians were killed in a general massacre which resembled the one that had heralded the opening of the Herero uprising, except that this time more of the settlers received timely warnings and were able to seek the protection of German stations.

Shortly after the Witboois raised the standard of revolt, about one-half of the remaining tribes in South West Africa joined them. The first tribe to cast its lot with the Witboois was the Franzmannschen Hottentots led by Simon Kopper. A few days later the Red Nation followed suit. By the end of October the Feldschuhträgers, under the leadership of Hans Hendrik, also joined the rebels. The Topnaars and Zwartboois wavered, but before they could act, quick-thinking German officials managed to disarm them. The Bondelzwarts were eager to join the battle, but because most of their leaders were imprisoned and they had no arms, they were powerless. The Baster Captain Hermanus van Wyk remained loyal to the Germans, as did

6. *Ibid.*, II, 13.

Captain Christian Goliath of Beersheba, Captain Paul Fredericks of Bethanie, and Captain Cornelius. The total number of able-bodied men opposing the Germans was rather less than 1500, and only a minority of these were equipped with modern rifles.

Tribe	Low estimate of fighters	High estimate
Witboois	800	900
Franzmannsche Hottentots	120	120
Red Nation	190	190
Feldschuhträgers	150	200
Total	1260	1410

The German garrisons in Namaland at the time of the outbreak of the rebellion numbered about 500, while the total German contingent in South West Africa in late 1904 was close to 10,000 men—well-equipped, well-trained, and for the most part unemployed. Yet despite their overwhelming numerical superiority, it took the Germans four frustrating years to pacify Namaland.

There were several reasons for the humiliating inability of the Imperial German Army to defeat the Hottentots. First, at the outbreak of the fighting there was no railroad into Namaland, and the German army, like all European armies, had become almost totally dependent on railroads. Lacking any rail link, the Germans were obliged to haul all their supplies from Lüderitz Bay to Keetmanshoop (a distance of 150 miles) along the so-called Baiweg trail. From Lüderitz Bay to Kubub the Baiweg crossed the Namib, a waterless desert of drifting sand. One veteran wrote that the trail was marked only by the carcasses of beasts of burden which had expired along the way. To cover the 150 miles took an average of 25 days. To supply a few hundred men was a major operation; to supply thousands was clearly an impossibility. The Witboois banked on the inaccessibility of Namaland to discourage the Germans.

The logistical problems created by the lack of a railroad

would have been alleviated to a considerable degree if the Hottentots had adopted the tactics of the Hereros and fought in pitched battles; but they chose instead to fight a guerrilla war, and this multiplied the Germans' problems tenfold. The very sparseness of their numbers made the Hottentots almost invisible. Time and again the Germans thought they had surrounded a Hottentot force only to have it disappear before they could bring their superior firepower to bear. Furthermore, British territory offered a tempting sanctuary to any Hottentot band that was too hard pressed. The few dozen British border patrols who had to watch hundreds of miles of border were powerless to stop violations of the frontier.

The initial German response to the Hottentot uprising was to send large-scale reinforcements to the south in hopes of nipping the rebellion in the bud. By the end of October six companies and one and one-half batteries were already on their way to the south under the command of Colonel Deimling. By January 1905 about 4300 officers and men and 2800 horses had arrived in Namaland, both from the north and from Germany. Von Trotha insisted repeatedly that the government should begin the construction of a railroad from Lüderitz Bay to the interior as soon as possible. His request was turned down by the authorities in Berlin, who were confident that the uprising would be put down long before the railroad could be completed. This decision added at least two years to the fighting, for the German forces were constantly hamstrung by lack of supplies.

The initial German operations were, on paper at least, reasonably successful. In December Deimling surprised Hendrik Witbooi in his camp at Naris, and after a short skirmish the Hottentots fled in panic leaving fifty bodies on the field of battle. German losses were three dead and nine wounded. Having captured the Hottentot camp, Deimling gave chase to the enemy but failed to make any further contact. The victory at Naris was, as modern strategists say, counterproductive, because it convinced the Hottentots that their best plan was to avoid pitched battles, in which German artillery and machine guns would be decisive. Instead, they relied on hit-and-run tactics to keep the Germans off balance. The southern part of

South West Africa, crisscrossed by deep gorges and dotted with mountain masses, was ideally suited for such operations.

The Hottentot revolt was an unpleasant surprise for von Trotha, because it raised doubts about the efficacy of policies of extermination. Rather than cowing the Hottentots, the destruction of the Hereros had stirred them to revolt. The reports of the Hottentot revolt caused a "profound depression" in government circles, according to the *Times,* and their reporters added that the Social Democrats received the news with "ill-disguised elation."[7] Men returning from the war were quoted in German newspapers as saying that two years at least would be required to pacify the colony. Even the editor of the conservative organ *Kreuzzeitung* suggested that perhaps the original acquisition of South West Africa had been a mistake. The sluggish response to the recruiting drive launched in late October in Germany suggested the general sense of despondency that pervaded the people. As a scapegoat Leutwein was cashiered, although his share in the fault was slight. Furthermore, the Kaiser decorated von Trotha with the First Class of the Order of the Prussian Crown with Swords—a sure sign that all was not going well. On December 5, 1904, the German government issued a pamphlet blaming the Hottentot uprising on the "arrogance" of the natives.

Despite the fact that Deimling did succeed in defeating Hendrik and driving him from his camp, von Trotha was unwilling to pursue an active military policy at least for the moment. Several factors conspired to make him cautious about pushing on with the campaign. First, there was the ever-present problem of logistics, but beyond that the German army in South West Africa in late 1904 was weakened by disease, was scattered about in a large number of posts and forts, and much of it was still occupied in putting out the last embers of the Herero revolt. Given the health of the troops and the manifold commitments the army had assumed, von Trotha believed that for the time being at least he did not have the resources necessary to pacify the south.

7. *Times* (London), October 20, 1904.

Deimling, the local commander in the south, considered von Trotha's evaluation of the situation completely false; he thought he had enough men to deliver a series of sharp attacks that would break the enemy's spirit and end the rebellion. Von Trotha argued that such piecemeal actions, reminiscent of Leutwein's campaign of the first weeks of the Herero War, were costly, time-consuming, and ineffective. Nevertheless, Deimling as the commander on the spot was able to put his own ideas into action. On January 2, 1905, three German columns converged on the Witbooi main body, which was then encamped in the Auob valley. After three days of heavy fighting, the Witboois withdrew and Deimling claimed a victory. The Witboois, far from being defeated, had simply retreated into the Kalahari desert, where Hendrik and his followers, who knew the desert well, would be able to remain as long as they chose. German losses were disconcertingly high—22 killed and 50 wounded and missing—considering that no significant advantage had been won. Having thus "defeated" the Witboois, Deimling regrouped his forces for an attack on Morenga, who was then encamped in the Karras hills. After a two-week campaign Deimling claimed a second victory. His report on the operations against Morenga is worth quoting, for it discloses Deimling's complete failure to comprehend the nature of the warfare in which he was engaged.

> Morenga's band has been routed and he has lost at least 130 dead. Morenga is no longer to be taken seriously as a factor; he has lost his cattle; he will never again succeed in forming a meaningful military band. Small groups will naturally reappear. The occupation forces left in the Karras hills, together with Langerke's troops, will keep them in hand by continuous observation and mopping up in the river valleys. . . . The myth which has grown up among all the Hottentots, even the Witboois, about the Karras hills and their impregnability has been finally smashed by our conquest. . . . Should the Witboois plan to withdraw into the Karras hills they will find that we have anticipated them. . . . One thing is certain to me since I have operated in the Karras hills, and that is that we could never again expect to enter into that area with so relatively few losses as we did this time because we caught the enemy by surprise.[8]

8. *Official History*, II, 88-89.

Deimling omitted from his report, probably because he did not
yet know it, that Morenga himself had been severely wounded
in the fighting.

Guerrilla Warfare

The situation in Namaland in March 1905 looked, on the
surface at least, to be quite hopeful to the Germans. Morenga
was wounded, and his followers had scattered. Hendrik Witbooi had been driven onto the desert and many of his followers
were demanding an end to the fighting. To bolster their spirits,
Stürmann, who had just returned from Hereroland, where he
had tried to make contact with the remnants of the defeated
Hereros, addressed the Witboois. According to one eyewitness,
he spoke as follows: "Cursed be those who believe that I am
only a Kaffir from Griqualand; cursed be those who do not
believe that God sent me. That all we have tried so far has failed
is because of your failure to believe, your disobedience, your
hesitancy. Now all that is over. You have been punished by
God. Why do you flee then? Is there any place in the world
where you can escape death?"[9] After speaking for some time in
this vein, Stürmann challenged his opponents to speak out
openly against him. Samuel Isaak, one of the leaders of the
tribe, took up the challenge and accused Stürmann of being the
source and cause of the troubles that beset the Hottentots. A
heated exchange followed, and was ended only after Hendrik
declared his complete confidence in Stürmann. So long as the
old chief gave his support to Stürmann, the war was destined to
continue. Deimling's campaign had not only not ended the
revolt, it had dispersed the enemy in such a way as to increase
greatly the difficulties the Germans would have in the future.
This von Trotha recognized, and as soon as he felt that the
north was completely secure, he headed south to take personal
command of the operations there. Clearly Deimling, whose
views were diametrically opposed to von Trotha's own, had
outlived his usefulness and in mid-March he was sent back to
Germany. On April 21, 1905, von Trotha himself arrived at

9. *Ibid.*, II, 64.

Gibeon and assumed command of the German force in Namaland. His first act was to issue a proclamation calling for the
immediate surrender of the rebels.

The mighty and powerful German Emperor will grant mercy to
the Hottentot people and will spare the lives of those who
voluntarily surrender. Only those who at the beginning of the
uprising murdered whites or ordered others to do so will forfeit
their lives in accordance with the law. I announce this to you
and further say that those few who do not submit will suffer the
same fate that befell the Hereros, who in their blindness believed
that they could carry on successful war with the mighty German
Emperor and the great German people. I ask you where are all
the Hereros today, where are their chiefs? Samuel Maharero,
who once called thousands of head of cattle his own, is now
harried like a wild beast and driven over the border into English
territory. He has become as poor as the poorest field Herero and
possesses nothing. It is the same with the other chiefs, the
majority of whom have lost their lives, and the Herero people
too have been annihilated—part of them dying of hunger and
thirst on the desert and part murdered by the Ovambos. The
Hottentots will suffer the same fate if they do not surrender and
give up their weapons. You should come with a white piece of
cloth on a stick together with your whole village and nothing
will happen to you. You will get work and receive food until the
war ends at which time the Great German Kaiser will regulate
anew the conditions in this land. He who believes that mercy
will not be extended to him should leave the land for as long as
he lives on German soil he will be shot—this policy will go on
until all such Hottentots have been killed. For the following
men, living or dead, I set the following price: Hendrik Witbooi—5000 marks; Stürmann—3000; Cornelius—3000; for the
other guilty leaders—1000 each.[10]

The opponents of the war in Germany had a field day vilifying
von Trotha's second proclamation, which in their opinion was
only marginally less offensive than the first. The German government, too, was not overly pleased by von Trotha's unerring
ability to put his foot in his mouth. The English newspapers
expressed amazement at the proclamation, which they took to
be a sign of weakness. In particular the English feared that
German ham-fistedness might succeed in stirring up a race war
in all of South Africa.

10. *Ibid.*, II, 186.

The practical consequences of the proclamation were all disastrous for the German cause. Not one Hottentot surrendered, and that fact surprised no one. One Hottentot chief, Cornelius, who up to that time had remained neutral (although some of his followers had joined in the fight), threw in his lot with the rebels upon finding that he had a price on his head. Finally, the German garrison guarding the Bondelzwarts prisoners at Warmbad misread von Trotha's intentions, and on the strength of their reading of the proclamation released their prisoners.

When it was clear that his proclamation had failed utterly to end the rebellion, von Trotha began to gather his forces for a military showdown. He planned to use the same general style of attack he had used at Waterberg—that is, a concentric attack aimed at total annihilation. Before this plan could be put into operation, however, von Trotha had to secure his lines of communication. This was not an easy task, particularly after Cornelius had entered the contest. In a series of lightning raids Cornelius had overrun a half dozen German outposts and spread a near panic among the local commanders. By these raids Cornelius had acquired enough ammunition, horses, and guns to pose a serious threat to the German rear. The flavor of this kind of warfare can be gleaned from an account that Cornelius himself gave of one of his raids carried out on April 7, 1905.

> When I heard that the German patrol had come from Bethanie, I attacked it. The patrol consisted of one officer and thirteen men. We were deployed at Gawaob and opened fire at 70 meters. The lieutenant sprang from his horse at once and gave orders. In a moment five of the riders fell. The lieutenant, in the meantime, pumped six shots from his weapon. When he was wounded in his left arm he started firing with his revolver and hit my brother Ruben in the back. Then he fell. He was a very brave man. As booty I got five guns. We got no horses as they were all killed. The lieutenant was not buried. I did not permit his body to be stripped.[11]

In April von Trotha concentrated most of his forces against Cornelius, but several weeks passed before the Germans made contact. Finally, on May 9, the Germans caught up with their

11. *Ibid.*, II, 108-109.

elusive foe—but only for a few fleeting moments. At the end of
the month the Germans again encountered Cornelius but again
he got away. In June Cornelius joined forces with Johannes
Christian, a Bondelswart chief who had just taken the field, and
Morris, an old ally of Morenga who had broken with him.

Unable to defeat Cornelius, von Trotha decided to try negotiations. Cornelius gives the following account of this effort.
"Morris rode up to me and reported that Lieutenant von Trotha
[the son of the German commander] wanted to speak to me. I
know the lieutenant well. He had been my commander in the
Herero campaign, and we had ridden together on many a
patrol. He had always been good to me. About dusk Trotha
arrived. When I said to him that Johannes Christian should be
present, he asked that he be summoned. We then tied our horses
to my wagon and sat down by the fire and began to talk. I was
very happy that Trotha was there. I believed that he came to
bring real peace. Trotha brought a letter from His Excellency
which said that nothing would happen to me if I would give up
my guns and ammunition."[12] While the two men were talking,
firing was heard. A German patrol was attacking the camp,
apparently unaware that von Trotha's son was there. Cornelius
shouted to von Trotha to stay close to him, fearing that in the
confusion he might be shot, but his warning was too late, for a
few moments later von Trotha was hit. "I rushed to him,"
wrote Cornelius, "but he was already dead; I spoke to him but
he understood me no more. I couldn't stay with him any longer
for already the bullets were whistling by me." Later Cornelius
found that one of his men had shot von Trotha believing that
he had been sent to set up the ambush.

After von Trotha's death, negotiations were broken off and
the Germans moved in for the kill. In a series of running battles
from June 27 to July 6 Cornelius's force was driven relentlessly
to the south, but before the Germans could deliver the coup de
grace they outran their supplies. By the end of the month,
however, the Germans had re-established contact with Cornelius's band. In August Cornelius slipped away from his pursuers

12. *Ibid.*, II, 118-119.

and escaped to the Karras hills, where he joined forces with Morenga. For almost three months Cornelius, with a force that never numbered more than 400 men, most of whom were armed with antiquated guns, successfully stood off the German forces, killing at least 50 of the enemy and wounding another 75.

While German forces were tied down in the pursuit of Cornelius, von Trotha tried to stall Morenga by offering him terms. In March, it will be recalled, Morenga had been badly wounded and his band scattered. For more than a month he disappeared from view, and the Germans hoped that perhaps that problem had been solved. On April 7, however, Morenga re-emerged in the role of cattle rustler, and it was clear that some action would have to be taken to prevent a recurrence of the cattle raids of the previous year. Accordingly, von Trotha sent Captain von Koppy accompanied by a Catholic priest, a non-com, and a native guide to find Morenga and try to induce him to surrender. The German terms were not very tempting—they offered no more than to spare his life if he surrendered—but Morenga was at least momentarily interested. He asked Koppy for time to consult with his allies, a request which was granted; twenty-four hours later, on April 25, Morenga sent word to the Germans that since his allies had refused the German offer, he himself was also rejecting it.

Upon hearing of Morenga's rejection, von Trotha sent four companies of mounted troops, two batteries of artillery, and a machine gun section into the Karras hills with orders to seek out the rebels and destroy them. Morenga abandoned his camp in the hills just a few hours before the Germans arrived, and he retreated to the eastern frontier. After hiding their weapons in the bush, Morenga and his men crossed the frontier into Bechuanaland, just ahead of the pursuing Germans. The British border guards were few in number and lax in attitude. Of the approximately 150 Hottentots that they took into custody on May 10, 1905, only five (by some accounts only two) reached Upington where they were to be interned. The rest drifted back across the border, recovered the weapons and ammunition they had hidden, and resumed their careers as cattle rustlers.

Two German companies were left in the eastern part of the

colony to watch for Morenga and his band. On June 15 one of these companies, commanded by Captain Erckert, surprised a group of Morenga's men as they were relaxing at their camp. The appearance of the Germans frightened off the Hottentots, and the Germans took possession of the camp and the cattle. Morenga turned this defeat into a victory two days later by using another camp and a herd of cattle as bait for a trap. He stationed a few men and a large number of cattle in the path of a German patrol; hidden in the bush around the camp was his main body. The Germans attacked the camp expecting another easy victory but were caught in heavy crossfire. For several hours they were completely cut off, and were saved from complete annihilation only by the timely arrival of a relief column. As it was, 19 Germans were killed and 31 wounded out of a force of 170. Though the editors of the German official history termed this action a "victory," the soldiers on the spot made no further effort to hinder Morenga's movement, and he returned unmolested to the Karras hills. There in his favorite haunt he re-established camp in June and a few weeks later was reinforced by the arrival of Cornelius's men.

Like Morenga's band, Hendrik Witbooi's followers disappeared after the March battles. The old warrior and his people trekked far out into the Kalahari, where they were relatively safe from the Germans. Occasionally a German patrol ventured into the desert, but for the most part the Germans were content to patrol the periphery of the desert hoping to prevent the Witboois from returning to their ancestral pasture lands around Gibeon. Though the desert provided a secure refuge for the Hottentots, life there was hard for both men and livestock, and the Witboois longed to return to the grasslands of the central plateau. In June Hendrik and his tribe eluded the German patrols and arrived unnoticed in the area around Gibeon.

The escape of the Witboois, combined with the continuing raids of Morenga and Cornelius, precipitated a serious crisis in leadership. The *Windhoeker Nachrichten* gave voice to the unhappiness prevalent among the settlers, who were dismayed at von Trotha's apparent inability to restore law and order to the colony. A colonial official reported to his superiors in

Berlin that "uncertainty reigns in every corner of the land."[13]
Von Trotha himself confessed that "the position is such that
a quick ending to the uprising cannot be anticipated." The
Times suggested that the situation had gone "from bad to
worse" and reported that the German government was considering the dispatch of 5000 more men in the hope that numbers alone would stabilize the situation. Just as Leutwein had
been blamed for the disasters of 1904, now von Trotha was
blamed for the disasters of 1905. The German newspapers,
except those of conservative persuasion, all joined in vilifying
the victor of Waterberg. The most charitable suggestion was
that the African sun had weakened his reasoning powers; the less
tolerant editors called him an "incompetent brute." It was
widely rumored that von Trotha had been de facto relieved, but
for reasons of prestige would be allowed to carry out one final
operation so that he would not have to return home in disgrace.
Even in the German ruling clique the continued frustration
caused serious tension. The *Kreuzzeitung*, a mouthpiece for
conservative landowners, noted in an editorial that the colonies
"had been acquired for the benefit of the German commercial
interests and for their sake alone are maintained at gigantic
cost."[14] The implication was clear: the conservatives were ques-
tioning whether the game was worth the candle. The left in
Germany, delighted to see the German army humbled, called
for a withdrawal of the army and its replacement by a colonial
police force.

Von Trotha, fully aware that not only his own reputation but
that of the army itself was at stake, decided that only a total
defeat of one of the enemies would remedy the situation. Since
Cornelius and Morenga were well dug in in the Karras hills,
von Trotha decided to attack the Witboois, who were placidly
tending their flocks in the vicinity of Gibeon. As a preliminary
to an attack, von Trotha sent a message to Hendrik calling for
his unconditional surrender. The old man answered that "peace
would be equivalent to my death and the extinction of my

13. Drechsler, *Südwestafrika*, p. 217.
14. Quoted in *Times* (London), August 22, 1905.

nation, for I know that there would be no sanctuary for me under your government."[15] Rebuffed in this effort, as he no doubt expected to be, von Trotha drew up his forces to deliver the coup de grace to the Witboois. Four columns were to converge on the Hottentots. In all, thirteen companies of mounted infantry (about 1500 men), twenty artillery pieces, and two machine guns were employed in the operation. At most, the Witboois numbered 750 men, and of course they had no weapons except rifles, and many of these were not modern types. On August 25, 1905, the concentric attack began. Resistance was almost nonexistent, and when the four columns approached the center point without having discovered any sizable body of Witboois, von Trotha reasoned that the foe must have escaped to the west. Consequently, the full German force was ordered to proceed west by forced marches to find and destroy the Witboois. Day after day the Germans plodded on, occasionally seeing a handful of natives, but usually without discerning any signs of life.

On September 19 Hendrik Witbooi and his men suddenly appeared, not to the west of Gibeon, but 200 miles to the south. On that day the Witboois fell on a German wagon train and captured it along with 1000 head of cattle. The German government, upon learning that von Trotha had failed once again, relieved him of his duties. Before he finally relinquished his command, however, von Trotha suffered further humiliations. On October 12, Morenga, who had been relatively quiet for several weeks, rode out of the Karras hills at the head of his band and overwhelmed the garrison of the German station at Jersualem, killing seven and capturing eight others. He sent the prisoners to von Trotha to tell the general that he, Morenga, had now decided to enter the fight in earnest. At the same time Hendrik Witbooi continued to roam about the southern part of the colony, looting and plundering at will.

On October 24, 1905, the Germans suffered their worst single defeat in the South West African campaign. On that day Lieutenant Koppy in command of four companies of mounted

15. Drechsler, *Südwestafrika*, p. 219.

troops was marching west along the northern bank of the Orange River in search of Morenga, who was reported to be in the area. At a place called Hartebeestmund, Koppy's troops were ambushed by Morenga, who had stationed his men both in the hills overlooking the German line of march and on an island in the Orange River. "The sand dunes were raked by the Hottentots while we saw nothing, absolutely nothing," wrote one of the survivors. "None of us could move at all without shots raining down on us. And the devils shot very well indeed! One after another fell to the right and the left."[16] Nightfall finally brought relief to the Germans, who escaped under cover of darkness. Forty-three men were killed, wounded, or missing that day; Morenga probably did not lose a man.

In February the anti-colonial sentiment, which had been vocal enough in June, became a howling chorus after the escape of Hendrik Witbooi. In a much-quoted open letter, a man who had served for many years in the colony wrote: "Next month it will be two years since the outbreak of the Witbooi uprising. This war is being conducted against people who possess neither money nor resources of their own. The greater portion of the material with which they wage war against us has been captured from us."[17] Against this gloomy appraisal of the situation, the synthetic optimism of Duke Johann Albrecht of Mecklenburg, who in addressing the congress in Berlin said that he expected that someday South West Africa would become "a glittering jewel in the crown of Germany" sounded forced indeed. As usual, the best indication of the seriousness of the situation was the hysterical distribution of honors. Three officers, including von Trotha, received the Pour le Mérite, the highest honor that the emperor could bestow. Furthermore, Deimling was ennobled for his services of the previous year.

The End of Witbooi Resistance

In the midst of this gloom, a shaft of sunlight appeared for the Germans—too late to save von Trotha, but still highly useful to

16. *Official History*, II, 239.
17. *Times* (London), October 20, 1905.

the government, which had to face an irate Reichstag on November 28. On October 29 Hendrik Witbooi was mortally wounded in a raid on a German supply train. His men managed to drag their chief to safety, but by the time they had escaped the Germans they found that the old man was near death from loss of blood. His final words were "It is enough. With me it is all over. The children should now have rest."[18] Von Trotha, ever generous to his foes, commented to the messenger who brought the news: "You couldn't have brought me a more beautiful message."

Though Isaak Witbooi was determined to continue the struggle despite the death of his father, his people were weary of the war and anxious to find peace. The peace party, headed by the sub-chief Samuel Isaak, made contact with a German representative on November 20 in order to arrange for the surrender of what remained of the tribe. The German conditions were simple: in return for their lives the Witboois were to turn over all guns, ammunition, and horses, and then the tribe would be settled at a camp near Gibeon. The Germans promised to provide food for the captives in return for which the Witboois were to work. Only those men guilty of murdering white settlers were to be punished. When Samuel Isaak heard the terms he pleaded for permission to keep some weapons. To this plea the German negotiator replied: "It is well that I have heard your intentions. You may now depart. On this day I say to you and your people: The German weapons will not rest until the last Witbooi, the last Bethanier, the last Bondelzwarts is under the earth. You alone can prevent this fate. We shall not again negotiate with you. Now go!"[19]

The German bluster worked, and Samuel meekly accepted the terms, little realizing that the Germans needed peace almost as much as his own people. The next day an impressive contingent of Hottentot warriors rode into the German camp at Berseba, "proud and upright, sitting on their horses with grim miens." In all 74 men, 44 women, and 21 children surrendered that day. It is instructive to note that the new governor, a ci-

18. *Official History*, II, 180.   19. *Ibid.*, II, 181.

vilian named Lindequist, thought the terms too lenient, while the new military commander, Colonel Dame, feared that the terms might be so harsh that the remaining Hottentots would go on fighting rather than accept them—something the soldiers wanted to avoid at all costs.

Dame's nightmare did not materialize. The remaining Hottentots surrendered on the same conditions granted to Samuel Isaak's people. On December 11, 1905, a second major surrender took place when 105 men and 172 women and children voluntarily submitted to the Germans. On December 24 another 50 men and 69 women and children gave themselves up. On March 2 the last major surrender took place when Cornelius led his people (86 men and 36 women and children) into German custody. With the surrender of Cornelius the last organized resistance of the Hottentots collapsed. Only the robber chieftain Morenga remained on the loose. Of the 1200 men who had originally joined Hendrik, 400 were in custody, and most of the remainder were either dead or interned on British soil. To conquer the Hottentots the Germans had deployed 15,000 men and suffered 1000 casualties.

The initial German attitude toward their prisoners was conditioned by that spirit of camaraderie which fighting men often feel toward their enemy after the battle. Major Maercker, one of the German officers present at the surrender of Samuel Isaak, gave the following account.

> The interrogation of Samuel Isaak was especially interesting for he made the most extraordinary impression and without being asked he gave his opinions on the psychological side of military leadership. Samuel Isaak had a disconcerting memory. He was exceptionally skilled in reading our military maps. During the interrogation his sense of humor came to the fore on several occasions especially since Samuel, who was speaking Dutch, fell back into high German whenever he became excited. When I asked him how many horses the Witboois had stolen in August 1905 at Malta heights, he answered quite seriously, "Major, in war one does not steal, one takes." A little later, however, he mentioned "stealing" water at Kirris East. When I asked whether he meant stealing or taking, he replied with a laugh: "No, in this case we stole, for we had to creep forward on all fours in order not to awaken the German guards!" On the next day when

he was translating a statement of Elias about the stealing of
some oxen, I corrected him by saying "taken," but he answered:
"No, that rascal steals."[20]

Though this lighthearted banter was the prelude to the many
long months of suffering and death which the Hottentots endured in German prison camps, its importance should not be
underestimated. The soldiers, harsh as they were, had little
interest in tormenting a defeated foe. The civilians, however,
both in the colony and in Berlin, had come to believe that only
by the total elimination of the native factor from South West
Africa could the colony be opened for white settlement and
civilization. The casualties suffered by the natives during the
fighting were the direct result of the military policy of the
Germans; those who died after the fighting were sacrificed to
the imperialist policies of the civilian government.

The Defeat of Morenga

When von Trotha set sail for Germany on November 17, 1905,
he believed that the war in South West Africa was all but over.
In the north the Hereros' resistance had been completely broken,
and in the south the Hottentots made no secret of their desire to
give up the struggle after the death of Hendrik Witbooi. Only
Morenga, with perhaps 400 men, was still in the field. Von
Trotha's confidence was quickly shown to be unwarranted.
Despite all German efforts, Morenga not only remained active
but grew stronger as the year wore on.

In December 1905 the German government had deluded itself
into believing that the long nightmare in South West Africa
was as good as over. On December 3, 1905, the new governor,
von Lindequist, ordered all military operations against the
hapless remnants of the Hereros to be stopped for a three-week
period, during which the survivors were ordered to present
themselves to either one of two concentration camps which had
been established to receive them. When he promulgated this
offer, 8000 Hereros were in German prison camps doing forced

20. *Ibid.*, II, 182.

labor, but many thousands more were still free, scratching out an existence from the land while avoiding German patrols. The German offer was tempting if for no other reason than that it meant food for the starving Hereros, and about 6000 of them accepted it. With the surrender of the last remaining free Hereros, the northern part of South West Africa was perfectly secure and ready for German colonization. In Lindequist's first public speech he called for a reconstruction program that would create in South West Africa "a massive and thoroughly German structure" which would become "a stronghold of the German race which Germans in South West Africa would look up to."[21] Peace, he assured his listeners, was at hand. The same confidence was echoed in Berlin. The emperor in opening the Reichstag in November told the members that "the latest report concerning the defeat of the Witboois justifies our hopes that peace will soon be at hand."[22] A few days later, in addressing the same body, Bülow spoke of military operations as if they were over, and said that rebuilding the shattered land would now take priority.

But beneath the optimistic rhetoric was an undertone of uneasiness, for Morenga was still unconquered and the rinderpest had reappeared. By the end of the year German veterinarians had controlled the rinderpest, but only by employing the drastic measure of slaughtering all the cattle in the affected area. The result of the slaughter was that the tenuous supply route from Lüderitz Bay to the interior was, for the moment, severed, leaving the German armies in Namaland without supplies. Until the supply routes were reopened Morenga was free to roam at will throughout the colony. The General Staff demanded that a temporary as well as a permanent solution be found for the crisis caused by the rinderpest. To alleviate temporarily the shortage of supplies, the generals asked for an additional 700 transportation troops, 2600 horses, and 1000 camels. With these men and beasts they hoped to start the flow of traffic moving again along the Baiweg trail from Lüderitz

21. *Times* (London), November 27, 1905.
22. Quoted in Schulthess, *Geschichtekalendar*, October 28, 1905.

Bay to the interior. Until the Reichstag voted the funds necessary to dispatch the men and animals demanded, the military authorities repudiated all responsibility for the safety of the troops in the field. Under this pressure the Reichstag obediently voted what the soldiers asked. But the generals knew that to reestablish the Baiweg route was at best a palliative; to solve the logistic problem once and for all, a railroad was needed. Though in May the Reichstag had refused to vote funds for any more railroad construction in South West Africa, the military renewed their request in December. The Reichstag bowed to the military demand this time, after Deimling warned the members that without a railroad from Lüderitz Bay to the interior "all progress made up to this point will be endangered."[23] Construction was begun in early 1906, but the line was not finished in time to play any role in the final pacification of the colony.

From December 1905 to January and February 1906, Morenga and his men raided almost at will in their favorite hunting grounds between the Karras hills and the Orange River. It was not until the arrival of the camels in February that the Germans were able to resume operations against him, and even then supplies were scanty enough to limit operations. Major Estorff, the commander of German troops in the Orange River area, opened his campaign against Morenga in late February. For this drive he deployed 13 companies of mounted troops, ten field pieces, and eight machine guns—a force not much smaller than von Trotha commanded at Waterberg when he was fighting 50,000 Hereros. Estorff divided his men into four sections commanded by Captains Erckert, Hornhardt, Siebert, and Heim. The four were to converge upon Morenga's men, who were encamped at a place called Kumkum on the Orange River. By March 4, all the Estorff men had reached their preliminary objectives and were ready to move in for the kill: all four units were to fall upon Morenga's men on March 13. Scouts kept Morenga well-informed of German movements. On March 8 he engaged the German column commanded by Siebert, which

23. *Verhandlungen des deutschen Reichstages*, 1904-1905, vol. 214, p. 84.

was marching up the Orange from the west, and delayed its progress enough so that Siebert failed to arrive at Kumkum as scheduled on March 13. On that day, in fact, only two of the four columns reached their objective of Kumkum; but even with only half his force, Estorff still greatly outnumbered Morenga. The battle, which was from the German side mostly fought with artillery, was largely bloodless and completely indecisive. After several hours of artillery fire the German infantry attacked, only to find that the enemy had abandoned their positions and disappeared to the north. Estorff's report to his superiors was a masterpiece of evasion. "Even if we can report no particularly impressive success against the enemy, who was bent on avoiding battle," he wrote, "still a meaningful step forward has been made in the struggle to suppress totally the uprising, and we must credit such progress as has been made to the splendid performance of the troops, which can only be properly evaluated by one who himself has known that area from personal experience."[24]

Having driven Morenga out of his camp on the Orange, Estorff set up a patrol line along the river as well as along the eastern boundary of the colony in an effort to prevent Morenga from escaping into British territory as he had done in the past. Because most of the available German troops were assigned to patrol duty, Morenga was free to move about the interior as he liked. On March 21 a small band of his men attacked the German station at Jerusalem, killing four of the guards and capturing all the horses. Five days later a German wagon train was captured after 11 of the 17 guards had been killed. On April 8 a German patrol was ambushed with the loss of 9 dead and 6 wounded. A week later another German post was overrun, one man killed and six wounded. In the whole history of the war there never was a month like the one that followed the German "victory" at Kumkum. Ten times Morenga's men struck and ten times they were successful. The whole German position in the southern part of the colony was shaken by a few score men, who were outnumbered at least twenty to one.

24. *Official History*, II, 274.

On May 4 Morenga's streak of victories ended. On that day he was encamped with 30 or 40 of his followers at a place called van Keois Vley when he was surprised by a superior German force. In the initial onslaught 16 of his followers were killed and in the subsequent pursuit 7 more fell. Morenga himself was badly wounded for the second time in the campaign, but he managed to make it across the frontier with 12 of his men. Though the defeat of Morenga eased the pressure on the Germans, it by no means ended it.

On May 16 two of Morenga's lieutenants, Johannes Christian and Morris, united their forces in the rugged land near the Lower Fish River. Three German columns converged on their camp, but the Hottentots escaped to the east. One patrol, consisting of seven officers and two men, retained contact with the fleeing enemy until on May 19 the Germans were ambushed with the loss of all men. Two days later the Hottentots attacked the German station at De Villierputz, killing three of the defenders but failing to take the station. On May 23 the German main body finally caught the Hottentots and drove them from an entrenched position, but there was no decision. By the end of May, four German companies commanded by Major Rentel were engaged in a fruitless pursuit of an elusive enemy. On May 24 the German station at Tsamab was overrun and all twelve men in the garrison killed. Arriving a few hours after the massacre, the German columns headed south down the Ham river in pursuit of the enemy. At Nukas the exhausted Germans finally caught up with the enemy, but after a brief skirmish they broke off the pursuit.

In the preceding eight days the German horsemen had ridden 230 kilometers through rugged and for the most part waterless country. While Rentel and his men were resting, Major Freyhold took up the pursuit, but his operations were no more successful. At one point Freyhold led his entire force into a trap from which he extricated them only after a sharp fight in which he lost 18 men. On June 21 the Germans suffered a further humiliation when a small Hottentot force boldly seized 118 horses and mules under the noses of their guards. This stroke immobilized the Eighth Battery of the imperial field artillery.

For four months the bands of Morenga, Johannes Christian, and Morris had quite literally run circles around the whole German army. The revolt which was thought to be all but over in December was still very much alive, and no one could doubt that for the moment at least the Hottentots had the initiative.

In the midst of these humiliations the Kaiser appointed his fourth commander-in-chief, Colonel von Deimling, who succeeded the hapless Colonel Dame. Deimling had been relieved of his command by von Trotha and sent back to the homeland under a cloud, but he nevertheless managed to establish himself as the semi-official government spokesman on South West Africa and expert-in-residence on all questions concerning the war. Though opponents of the war detested him as the very symbol of military arrogance, the Kaiser and the high command were inclined to see him as a prophet without honor. In the late autumn of 1905 when the war was at one of its many low points, von Deimling had been ennobled for his services; and now in the late spring of 1906, when the situation had passed into the realm of high comedy, Deimling was sent to retrieve whatever shred of honor was still retrievable. After conferring with Dame and Lindequist, Deimling officially assumed command on July 6, 1906.

When Deimling first had a command in South West Africa he favored the use of conventional military operations against the rebels, but time and experience had changed his mind. As a first step, he ordered a stop to the fruitless tactics of aimless pursuit and concentrated instead on means of cutting off the robber bands' means of support. The problem was, as Deimling saw it, that the Germans—both military and civilian—had too many livestock in the war area. These large herds were a constant temptation to the Hottentots, who supported themselves by stealing horses and cattle and then selling them to merchants across the Orange River in British territory. To stop this illicit traffic Deimling instituted drastic measures. First, all privately owned horses and cattle were removed from the danger areas and taken to safe pastures far to the north. Further, all excess military livestock was removed, and such horses and cattle as were deemed essential were concentrated in a few well-protected posts. Deimling hoped that by these measures he could force the Hottentots to attack German strength rather than German weakness, as they had been able to do in the past.

Having solved the livestock problem, Deimling reorganized his forces into a series of "flying squads," each with a specific area to protect. These flying squads were based at Ukamas, Warmbad, and Uhabis, as well as in the vicinity of the lesser and the greater Karras hills. According to Deimling's plan, each flying squad was to pursue the enemy only in its own territory; once the enemy passed beyond the line of demarcation, the next flying squad was to take over. Deimling hoped these measures would force the Hottentots to reveal their positions by attacking fortified posts, after which he would exhaust them by continuous pursuit.

On August 6, 1906, Johannes Christian with about 50 men attacked the German station at Alurisfontein, and Deimling's new tactics received their first test of battle. The German defenders drove off the Hottentots and a flying squad took up the pursuit. For the next ten days three successive German columns kept on the trail of the Hottentots. On August 18 the Germans finally caught up with their exhausted foe and defeated them in a sharp fire-fight. Thereafter the pursuit went on without respite until, on August 30, the Germans again caught up with the foe. This time they killed most of the survivors and captured almost all of their horses. For over three weeks Johannes Christian had been on the move, covering in that time 500 miles and fighting three battles. Four German columns had shared in the action and despite much hard riding the Germans were still relatively fresh. German losses had been moderate—6 dead, 2 missing, and 17 wounded—whereas the Hottentots had been almost annihilated.

During August two other Hottentot bands were subjected to the same harrying treatment. The success of the new tactics was clear. The Germans had seized the initiative, for the first time in many months. Cattle theft came to an end in August, and without a plentiful supply of cattle to steal the Hottentots were quickly reduced to near starvation. On October 25, 1906, Johannes Christian sent word to Deimling that he was ready to enter into negotiations. Deimling offered generous terms. In some cases he even offered to permit the rebels to keep their guns; in others he guaranteed the life and liberty of any man who surrendered.

On November 16, while the preliminary negotiations were underway, a small German force surprised a Hottentot band encamped on the Lower Fish River, killing some of them and driving the remainder into the bush. Though neither the Germans nor the Hottentots recognized it, this nameless battle was the last formal military operation of the great revolt. Almost three years to the day since the outbreak of the Bondelzwarts rebellion the colony was finally at peace. On December 21, 1906, a general meeting was held at Ukamas where a definitive peace was signed. One of the German negotiators, a Captain von Hagen, left the following impression of the final act.

I was constantly on the move between Ukamas and Heirachabis carrying on negotiations. The negotiations were very difficult and often passionate; it took the patience of Job to talk the Bondels out of their suspicions. On December 21 I rode to the last meeting and told the rebels that the pre-negotiations had ended and the final negotiations must take place at Ukamas on the 22nd. Johannes, accompanied by five of his lieutenants, came to us. Lieutenant Colonel von Estorff conducted the talks in person with exemplary calm and great shrewdness. His knowledge of the natives, the high esteem which he enjoyed with them, served the German cause well. On December 22, 1906, the [Hottentot] Captain agreed to giving up weapons, but objected to settling down in the vicinity of Keetmanshoop. Von Estroff gave him to the 23rd to think it over. Even on that day the Bondels remained adamant on the question of settling around Keetmanshoop. Under no conditions would they countenance a resettling, and they said they would fight to the last man rather than submit. Von Estorff therefore faced the question: Should he give in or not? If he remained firm the end of the war would be put off indefinitely. The matter of where the Bondels were settled appeared to him to be of little significance since he was under orders from Deimling not to let the negotiations flounder on this issue. He therefore granted their wishes and the treaty was signed that very evening.[25]

25. *Ibid.*, II, 294-295.

At dusk on December 23 the Bondels turned in their guns and then attended a church service with the Germans. "In the evening Father Malinowski held services in the small mission church. There the Bondels sat peacefully . . . the Father spoke movingly about the successful work of peace. To me personally it was a strange sensation to sit together in church with these people who had fought against us for three years and had killed so many of my comrades. During the service I had all the weapons which had been turned in loaded unobtrusively in a wagon and taken to Ukamas."[26] During January the remaining Bondels turned in their weapons and submitted to German rule. In Berlin many higher officials were unhappy with the terms of the peace, which they held to be excessively lenient, but as the Emperor put it: "The main point is that we got hold of their weapons and they are therefore helpless and can no longer shoot down my brave officers and men."

With the surrender of the Bondels only Simon Kopper and a handful of followers remained in the field, but they were far out in the Kalahari and posed no danger to the peaceful development of the colony. On March 31, 1907, the German government officially declared German South West Africa pacified. At the same time, orders went out to reduce German military strength to 4000 men under the command of von Estorff.

26. *Ibid.*, II, 295.

7
The Reckoning

THE TOTAL GERMAN LOSSES in South West Africa
from January 1904 to March 1907 amounted to about 2500 men
killed, wounded, and missing. Of this number about 100 were
civilians and 100 were marines; the remainder were soldiers.
The breakdown of army losses is as follows.[1]

	Officers	Men	Total
Losses in Action			
Dead	62	614	676
Missing	2	74	76
Wounded	89	818	907
Total	153	1506	1659
Died from Disease			
	26	663	689
Grand Total			2348

African losses cannot be determined with such precision. According to most experts, however, the Hereros numbered 80,000
at the time the rebellion began; in 1911 only 15,130 were still
alive. What happened to the missing 65,000? A few, to be sure,
had escaped into British territory, but the overwhelming majority were dead. Some died in battle; more perished on the Omaheke wastes; additional thousands were slaughtered by German
patrols who hunted them down like wild beasts all during 1905;
a good many died in the concentration camps. Hottentot losses
were not quite so devastating. In 1904 there were believed to

1. See source note to Table 2, Chapter Four.

have been about 20,000 Hottentots in the colony; seven years later that number had been reduced to 9781.[2] As in the case of the Hereros, battle losses probably accounted for only a small fraction of the total loss. Many died of disease, more died in prison camps. When Deimling took command of the German forces in South West Africa, he ordered all Hottentot prisoners, numbering just under 1800, to be transferred from the interior to an island off the coast for greater security. In April 1907 only 245 survivors of this group remained, and of these only 25 were rated as capable of working.

The German government, not content with decimating the tribes, was determined to reduce the handful of survivors to the status of semi-servitude. On August 18, 1907, the Colonial Office issued orders which defined the position of the native in South West Africa.[3] No native could own either land or cattle (the Ovambos were an exception); all males over seventeen had to carry passes; vagrancy (defined as not having a job) was a punishable offense; and all natives were subject to forced labor. The Colonial Office ordered local officials to apprehend all unregistered natives and force them to work. Servants whose work was deemed unsatisfactory by their masters could be turned over to local government officials for punishment, which customarily took the form of whipping. In a single year (1911-1912), 1655 official whippings were administered, but this figure represented only the tip of the iceberg, for masters had almost unlimited power to administer corporal punishment to their servants. Government reports are studded with cases of gross mistreatment of natives. A farmer named Kramer, for instance, was haled into court for using excessive violence on his servants. Among other things he was said to have whipped a man "all afternoon" and a woman "all evening." In all, he was charged with abusing seven women and one man. Two of the women died. He was sentenced to 21 months in prison, but the sentence was subsequently reduced to 4 months.[4] Nor was Kra-

2. Drechsler, *Südwestafrika*, pp. 242ff.
3. Wellington, *South West Africa*, pp. 229ff.
4. See *Report on the Natives of South West Africa and their Treatment by Germany* (London, 1918) for a detailed account of the horrors.

mer an exception. There were many other cases of German brutality recorded in the files. Most disinterested observers— including the first Colonial Secretary, Dernburg—were convinced that mistreatment of natives remained a severe problem up to the outbreak of the First World War.

Though the Africans suffered in the period following the uprising, the colony prospered. In 1908 diamonds were discovered along the coast, and for the first time South West Africa had a profitable export. Partly because of the diamonds, partly because of government subsidies, immigrants came to the colony in record numbers after 1907. The white population rose from 3000 in 1906 to 14,000 at the outbreak of the war. By 1914 it was clear that European culture had triumphed; civilization had come to South West Africa. The native factor had been reduced to a few thousand cowed creatures serving their white masters.

By European standards the behavior of the Germans in South West Africa could be described as at best harsh and as at worst sadistic. Who can explain how supposedly civilized men could drop the attributes of civilization so quickly? The easy answer would be to argue that Germans are Germans and have a propensity to barbarism, but this answer is far from satisfying. In the first place, the Germans were not the only Europeans to use their subject people cruelly. The French—in Madagascar, in Equatorial Africa, and in Indo-China—had suppressed uprisings with methods which, if lacking the heavy-handedness of the Germans, were not much less cruel. The Belgians in the Congo, the Americans in the Philippines, the Dutch in the East Indies, and the Japanese in Korea all had used the machine gun, the whip, and forced labor to bring their subjects to heel. Even the British could be ruthless when they thought it served their interests. The general European attitude can find no more eloquent expression than in the Report of the Commissioners into the Administration of the Congo State. In 1904, under intense international pressure, King Leopold had appointed a three-member commission to investigate the allegations that the Belgians had used means repugnant to civilized men in ruling the Congo Free State. After cataloguing repeated instances of shocking mistreatment of the native population, the commissioners came to what now seems a rather remarkable conclusion: although such conduct was not exemplary, in the ruling of "inferior races" forced labor was "absolutely necessary" in order to bring the natives along the road to civilization. "In a word, it is by this basis alone that the Congo can enter into the pathway of modern civilization and the population be reclaimed from its natural state of barbarism."[5] The Germans may have been more callous than their European neighbors, but their techniques were those used by all the colonial powers.

The brutality of the Germans flowed, then, from European folk customs and was not unique to the Germans. The idea of racial superiority, the contempt for native life styles and lives, were part of a belief in the civilizing mission of the white man. This confidence that Europeans had in their mission, as well as in themselves, was reinforced by the undoubted material, technological, and scientific achievements of their society; and it was reinforced by their feelings toward the blacks, which ranged from patronizing contempt to physical repulsion. Despite the high-sounding phrases about a "civilizing mission," most of the whites were only interested in the black man for his labor.

When the labor of the black man was no longer needed, the Germans were quite frank in admitting that the best, and indeed perhaps the only solution, would be "extirpation." So prevalent was this idea that on March 23, 1905, the head of the Colonial Department, Prince Hohenlohe, felt compelled to assure the members of the Reichstag that the government had no intention of "exterminating" the blacks.[6] Quite the contrary, he said, we consider them our most valuable economic asset. After the war, Hohenlohe assured the house, the natives would be settled on reserves and there trained to work. But despite Hohenlohe's assurances, the work of extirpation was going on, limited only by the colony's need for sufficient manpower to recover.

In this orgy of death it is not the ruthlessness of the soldiers or the viciousness of the settlers that is so shocking; rather it is

5. Quoted in *Times* (London), November 6, 1905.
6. Drechsler, *Südwestafrika*, p. 262.

the cold-blooded efficiency of the bureaucrats. They knew all the revolting details of the slaughter, and they had the power to stop it; but while not actually condoning what was going on, they passively allowed the reign of terror to run its course unchecked. The colonial official saw in the elimination of the natives the quickest and most efficient solution to the problem of ruling South West Africa. Without natives the land could be settled by Germans and ruled as German territory. It seemed to them a sensible solution that removed a number of otherwise knotty problems. When two minor officials in the colonial office brought to the attention of their superiors evidence of widespread misdeeds on the part of German officials in the colonies, their reports were quietly filed and no action was taken. When the two officials persisted, they were forced to retire on grounds of "mental incapacity." Ultimately these officials leaked the information to a sympathetic member of the Reichstag, who presented the documents to Chancellor von Bülow himself. Bülow showed little interest in the crimes of the colonial officers, but he was horrified at the unauthorized leakage of information. He ordered disciplinary proceedings to be taken at once against the officials.[7]

For two years, from 1904 to 1906, the anti-colonial forces—a loose alliance of the Socialists, the Center, and the Radicals—had a majority in the Reichstag. Time and again the anti-colonialists embarrassed the government by voting down budgetary requests. Then in December 1906 Bülow dissolved the house and went to the country asking for a mandate to carry on the colonial mission. In the only election campaign in European history fought exclusively on imperial issues, the anti-colonial forces suffered a severe electoral setback. The German people reversed the trend of the preceding three decades, turning against the left and giving the colonial parties a massive mandate. Bülow took a record of inhuman cruelty and military failure to the people, and the people endorsed imperialism by a great majority.[8]

7. Klaus Epstein, "Erzberger and the Colonial Scandals," *English Historical Review* (LXXIV, 1959), pp. 647ff.

8. See George Crothers, *The German Elections of 1907* (London, 1937).

So the victory was won and a peace, the peace of a graveyard, settled over South West Africa.

It remains only to consider how the German army managed to perform so poorly. The geography of South West Africa is, of course, part of the answer, but though South West Africa was not the best place in the world to carry on a war, neither was it the worst; and besides, one might expect that professional soldiers, given three years, would be able to adapt themselves at least in part to a novel situation. The General Staff itself gave explanations which, while no doubt convincing to the officer corps, have a whining tone that failed to impress the civilian mind. In their official reports to the Reichstag, the army command emphasized the supply difficulties, the roughness of the terrain, the strain on soldiers who had to fight for months on end without proper rest. Lurking just beneath the surface in these documents is the accusation that the Reichstag, by not voting all that the military asked, was the real culprit. The army's opponents blamed the generals, accusing them of incompetence, claiming that they were too rigid, too slow to adapt to new challenges—in a word, calling them bunglers.

There is more than a little truth in the charges leveled against the German army on the record of its performance in South West Africa, but after a generation of experience with guerrilla warfare, modern judgment tends to be more lenient toward the generals. Militarily, they were faced with a difficult task, much more difficult than even they were willing to admit. Their men were not trained to fight guerrillas and their equipment was often ill-fitted for use against a lightly armed but highly mobile enemy. Before 1914 all armies were far too dependent on railroads to permit them to operate effectively at any appreciable distance from them. This dependence on the railroad seriously compromised the mobility of the forces in the field. Artillery, machine guns, and rapid-fire rifles gave the Germans overwhelming superiority in firepower, but it was purchased at a high cost, for it tied the German soldiers to a bulky, slow-moving, and highly vulnerable supply train, without which their weapons were useless.

But the problems of the German army transcended the merely

technical, and were often conceptual as well. The German army was conceived of as an instrument to engage in combat with similar instruments—that is, with aggregates of men uniformed, disciplined, equipped, and commanded in a manner similar to the German army. Victory in battle was looked upon as the logical goal of military action, and all generals knew that victory was achieved when the corporate will of the enemy was broken; that is, when the individuals who made up the enemy army were atomized and fragmented to the point where coordinated action was no longer possible. United, an army is strong, but when the inner cohesion that binds the army together is dissolved, then the individuals count for nothing. European military theorists as well as the generals in the field knew that the way to break the corporate will of the enemy is to use a combination of firepower and maneuver. Victory is won by breakthroughs or flanking attacks. When the flank of an army is turned or, better yet, when its rear is exposed, that army is as good as beaten. These hoary truths had been taught for generations in every military college and staff school in Europe.

In guerrilla warfare, however, the tactics and strategy of the military manuals were almost always worthless, and often counterproductive. When the German army came to South West Africa it found no enemy army, only an enemy people. The distinctions between a fighting man, a cattle rustler, and a peaceful shepherd were blurred and generally arbitrary. Furthermore, to outflank the enemy, to encircle his positions, to break his line, were in most cases not recipes for victory but invitations to disaster. "Victory" in guerrilla warfare only breaks up the enemy into smaller units, thereby multiplying the problems of the victor. Thus it was that most German victories—and it is instructive to remember that the Germans claimed to have won practically all the 200 battles fought during the three years of the war—either did not improve the German position or materially worsened it. The repeated frustrations of the German commanders finally drove them to pursue a war of annihilation. They rightly saw that the only effective way to break the will of the enemy was to kill so many of them that the few survivors would submit to their rule.

Victory, then, could be obtained only by terror—terror on a massive scale, terror which spared neither old nor young, neither children nor non-combatants. There were individuals within the army who shrank from a policy directed as much against babes-in-arms as against enemy soldiers; but before long most of the soldiers acquired a taste for blood—often stimulated by real or imagined enemy atrocities—and the civilized inhibitions faded. The Germans, like many nations before and after, were trapped in the paradox of power. On the one hand, they had almost unlimited ability to do violence to their enemies. But on the other, all their cannons, all their machine guns, all their well-drilled soldiers, all their tactical skills, and all their money could not enable them to impose their will upon a handful of nearly powerless people. They learned to their dismay that even "black savages" would sometimes rather die as free men than live as slaves. For all their power, they could kill but not convince.

Appendix:
The Peace of
Okahandja

The terms of the peace which was signed on September 23, 1870, are of considerable interest for they demonstrate the sophisticated sense that the tribes had of the nuances of inter-tribal relations. (Published in the Cape by Government Notice No. 470 of 1870, together with Annexes.)

TREATY OF PEACE

23 September 1870

Treaty of Peace between the Chiefs of Hereroland, to wit: Kamaherero, the Paramount Chief, a number of other Chiefs, and minor Chiefs, and Abraham Swartbooi, Kaptein of the Namaqua tribe of Rehobothers, at present residing in the vicinity of Bokberg (all of the abovementioned Herero Chiefs), all on the one side,

and

Jan Jonker Afrikaner, Kaptein of the Afrikaners, on the other side.

There were absent, of the war making parties on the Herero nations' side, the (powerful) Chief Kambazembi, and nineteen other Chiefs, who were prevented from coming.

On the side of the Namaqua Kapteins who had not yet asked for peace there were absent, Vleermuis, Kaptein of Amraal's tribe, Barnabas (Kaptein of the Red Nation), and Karl Hendrik (Kaptein of the Veldskoendraers).

The three Kapteins of Great Namaqualand, David Christian of Bethanie, Jacobus Izaak of Berseba, and Kido Witbooi of

Gibeon, arrived on the 14th and 17th of September, 1870, in order to be present at the Peace Conference to be held at Okahandja, and as impartial Kapteins to confirm the Peace by their presence, having been invited thereto by both parties.

On 27 May 1870, a meeting had already taken place between the Paramount Chief Kamaherero, the Chief Aponda, and a few other Herero Chiefs and Jan Jonker Afrikaner, when they mutually agreed to a cessation of hostilities and to be friends until the Great Meeting.

On 23 September 1870 the peace making parties, after several discussions, came to a decision on the following points:

1. That a sincere peace between the Hereros and the Afrikaner tribe is established and shall be maintained.
2. That peace shall also be granted to the beforementioned absent Namaqua Kapteins, who had taken part in the war, in case they shall ask for it.
3. That the Herero Chiefs, give by way of loan, to Jan Jonker Afrikaner, the place called Windhoek, for himself and his people to live in, with a missionary of the Rhenish Society.
4. That Kaptein Jan Jonker Afrikaner has obtained no right whatsoever to interfere or meddle with the affairs of the Herero people or their land nor with foreigners living in or traveling among them.
5. That the peaceable Namaqua Kapteins present, as well as the Kaptein Jan Jonker Afrikaner, ensure that the thoroughfare to and from the Cape Colony may be traveled again in safety.
6. That the Herero prisoners of war at present in Great Namaqualand shall obtain their freedom, and in case they themselves shall desire to return to their own country, the Namaqua Kapteins will assist them therein.
7. That all goods and properties taken during the war by the respective war parties shall remain in possession of the present holders; and
8. That no Kaptein shall have the right to forbid travelers or traders from passing on to other peaceable tribes or countries, or turn them back.

OKAHANDJA, 23. 9. 1870

Peace Mediating Kapteins
David Christian
Jacobus Izaak
Kido Witbooi

Chiefs of the Herero Nation
Kamaherero (Paramount)
Zeraua
Aponda
Katjihuiko
Kaviujoko
Tjetjo
Kauambaauo
Katjinoujungu

Kaptein of the Rehobothers (not the Basters)
Abraham Swartbooi

Kaptein of the Afrikaners
Jan Jonker Afrikaner

As Witnesses to the Above Signatures
C. H. Hahn
Ph. Diehl
C. Conrath

in fidem copiae
C. H. Hahn, Superintent

Bibliographic Essay

There are several good general accounts of South West African history. The best general history is John H. Wellington, *South West Africa and its Human Issues* (Oxford, 1967). For an analysis of the colonial administration, there is Helmut Bley, *Kolonialherrschaft und Sozialstruktur in Deutsch-Südwestafrika* (Hamburg, 1968). The only comprehensive history of the German Colonial Empire is the outdated study by Mary E. Townsend, *The Rise and Fall of Germany's Colonial Empire 1884-1918* (New York, 1930). Recent first-rate monographs on German South West Africa include the following: H. Drechsler, *Südwestafrika unter deutscher Kolonialherrschaft* (Berlin, 1966); R. First, *South West Africa* (London, 1963); I. Goldblatt, *History of South West Africa* (Cape Town, 1971); F.F. Müller, *Kolonien unter der Peitsche* (Berlin, 1962); M. Nussbaum, *Von "Kolonialenthusiasmus" zur Kolonialpolitik der Monopole* (Berlin, 1962); Heinrich Loth, *Die Christliche Mission in Südwestafrika* (Berlin, 1963); J. Baumann, *Mission und Oekumene in Südwestafrika* (Leiden, 1965); W.O. Henderson, *Studies in German Colonial History* (London, 1962). The classic account of German South West Africa during the nineteenth century is H. Vedder, *South West Africa in Early Times* (Oxford, 1938). None of these works, however, touches upon the military campaign in more than a casual way. The major primary source for the military operations is *Die Kämpfe der deutschen Truppen in Südwestafrika* (2 vols., Berlin, 1907), based on official materials and written by the Military History Section of the German General Staff. In addition, the General Staff submitted to the Reichstag periodic reports on the progress of the campaign, and these have been printed as *Anlage* to the Reichstag debates. The volumes of the Reichstag debates for the period of the war (*Stenographische Berichte über die Verhandlungen des Reichstages* (Berlin, 1844-) contain much useful information about German attitudes toward the war. The Colonial Office published a weekly magazine entitled *Deutsches Kolonialblatt*, in which summaries of military action, official dispatches, and occasional eyewitness accounts are to be found. In 1918 the British Government published *Report on the Natives of South West Africa and their Treatment by Germany* (London, 1918). It is a storehouse of horror stories, taken for the most part from German colonial records. Besides the official records, there are a number of accounts written by participants. Among the most useful of these are the following: M. Bayer, *Mit Hauptquartier in Deutsch-Südwestafrika* (Berlin, 1909); B. von Deimling, *Südwestafrika, Land und Leute* (Berlin, 1906); H. Alverdes, *Mein Tagebuch aus Südwest* (Oldenburg-Leipzig, 1906); Franz von Bülow, *Im Felde gegen die Hereros* (Bremen, 1905); Karl Dove, *Deutsch-Südwestafrika* (Berlin, 1913); A. von François, *Die Hottentotten-Aufstand* (Berlin, 1905); Theodor Leutwein, "Der Aufstand in Deutsch-Südwestafrika," *Deutsche Revue* (1907); Leutwein, *Elf Jahre Gouverneur in Deutsch-Südwestafrika* (Leipzig, 1912); Paul Rohrbach, "Südwestafrika," in *Deutsche Kolonialwirtschaft* (2 vols., Berlin, 1907); Kurt Schwabe, *Der Krieg in Deutsche Kolonialwirtschaft* (2 vols., Berlin, 1907), *Der Krieg in Deutsch-Südwestafrika* (Berlin, 1907), and *Mit Schwert und Pflug in Deutsch-Südwestafrika* (Berlin, 1904); and Else Sonnenberg, *Wie es am Waterberg zuging* (Berlin, 1905).

Although important historical source materials that deal specifically with the African societies of South West Africa exist, they have been treated as minor and peripheral components of the European colonial historiography. For example, none of the major figures of the tribal units—such as Morenga, Hendrik Witbooi, and Samuel Maharero—has been the subject of a satisfactory biography, even though there is sufficient information for the writing of one. On the other hand, historical studies of African societies in the larger Southern African region (which includes the modern Republic of South Africa, Rhodesia-Zimbabwe, and the semi-independent states of LeSotho, Swaziland, and Botswana) have been numerous and impressive over the past decade or so. See, for example, L. M. Thompson, editor, *African Societies in Southern Africa: Historical Studies* (New York, 1969). Many of the themes and issues that characterize these studies of Southern Africa's Bantu and Khoi populations are also pertinent to South West Africa, at least insofar as they assist in the development of a comparative perspective.

The African historical background to tribal warfare in nineteenth-century Southern Africa is carefully treated in M. Wilson and L. M. Thompson, *The Oxford History of South Africa*, Volume I (Oxford, 1969), especially Chapter IX, pp. 391-405. On the issue of the motivations that inspired African resistance and rebellion, two works by T. O. Ranger—*Revolt in Southern Rhodesia 1896-7* (London, 1967) and "Connexions between 'primary resistance' movements and modern mass nationalism," *Journal of African History*, IX, 3-4 (1968)—are of fundamental importance. On broader patterns of resistance and rebellion throughout the African continent, one may consult R. I. Rotberg and Ali A. Mazrui, editors, *Protest and Power in Black Africa* (New York, 1970). An instructive case study from neighboring South Africa is M. Hunter (Monica Wilson), *Reactions to Conquest* (London, 1936). The work of J. Iliffe and other scholars who have studied the *maji maji* rebellion against German rule in Tanganyika (an event which parallels in time and in many of its central features the Herero Rebellion) is summarized in Iliffe's "Tanzania Under German and British Rule," in B. Ogot, editor, *Zamani: A Survey of East African History* (Nairobi, new edition, 1974), pp. 295-313. C. Miller's *Battle for the Bundu: The First World War in East Africa* (New York, 1974) also treats many of the themes and issues found in the South West African case.

Major biographical studies of Southern African resistance figures are G. Shepperson and T. Price, *Independent African* (Edinburgh, 1956), and L. M. Thompson, *Survival in Two Worlds: Moshoeshoe of LeSotho, 1786-1870* (Oxford, 1975). Finally, the curiously one-dimensional views of the missionary role in European colonization and conquest in Southern Africa are being greatly modified by modern historical scholarship; as a prime example, see J. S. Galbraith, *Reluctant Empire* (Berkeley, 1963).

Index

Hereros, 31-34 *passim*, 38, 41, 42, 44, 47, 49, 51-54 *passim*, 56-65 *passim*, 70-72 *passim*, 100; geographical factors concerning, 9; knack for finding water, 12; Bantu tribe, 14; appearance and character of, 16, 20; culture and language of, 17; political organization of, 18; social differentiation among, 19; nine tribes of, 19-20; power of chief of, 20; and regard for treaties and law, 20-21; number of tribes of, 25; and terminology, 29; and natural and man-made disasters, 50; equipment and manpower of, in opposition to Germans, 67-68; meeting of headmen of, 69; first attacks of, 73, 74-78 *passim*; German response to initial attack of, 80, 81, 84-87, 88, 89; victories of, 92; conflict of, with Glasenapp, 98-99, 100; and battle of Onganjira, 102, 103; and result of March-April battles, 105, 106-108, 109; amnesty offered to, 112; and preliminaries to battle of Waterburg, 113, 114; and Waterburg campaign, 115, 117-122, 124-131, 132, 136, 137, 139, 142-145 *passim*, 147, 155-157 *passim*; compared to ancient Germans, 121; estimate of total losses of, 164, 165
Herero wars: first, 33; second, 34; third ("War of Freedom"), 37; fourth, 38, 44-45; end of first phase of, 104
Heyde, von der, 115, 122, 124
Heydebreck, von (Second Mountain Battery), 94, 127
Historians, German official: quote, 131; concerning death of Burgsdorff, 139; editors' report, 149
Hoachanas, peace of, 36, 47
Hohenlohe, Prince, 167
Hornhardt, Captain, 157
Hornkranz, 20, 45, 46
Hottentots (Namas), 9, 70, 71, 72, 78; location of, 22, 23; Bereseba and Bethanie, 24; number of tribes of, 25; derivation of name of, 28, 29; early survival of, 31-33; leadership of, 36; and conflict with Hereros, 37, 39; Hendrik's vision for, 44; Khauas, 47, 48; Franzmannschen, 48, 139; Bondelzwarts, 63, 64, 84; revolt of, 132, 134, 135-139, 142-149 *passim*, 151-155 *passim*, 159-163 *passim*; estimate of number of, opposing Germans, 140; strategy of, 141; total losses of, 164-165

imperialism, German, 39
Isaak, Samuel, 144, 153, 154

Jerusalem, German station at, 151, 158
Job, reference to, 162
Jonker, Jan, 33-36, 43

"Kaffirs," 135, 144
Kaiser, German, 48, 63, 87, 147, 156, 160, 163; message of, to Estorff, 96-97; message of, to von Trotha, 126; request from Bulow to, 130-131; von Trotha decorated by, 142; proclamation calling for surrender of rebels by, 145
Kajata, chief, 108
Kakimena, 20, 49
Kalahari desert, 12, 143, 149, 163
Kalfontein, 127, 138
Kamaherero, 41, 42
Kambasembi, 65
Kambazeni, Chief, 20
Kanduwe, 98
Kaokoveld, 32
Karibib, town of, 77, 78, 120
Karras Hills, 63, 64, 138, 143, 148-149, 150, 151, 157, 161
Karupuka, 118
Keetmanshoop, 64, 66, 138, 140, 162
Kehoro, 98
Keois Vley, 159
Khaynach (NCO), 119
Khauas. *See* Hottentots, Khauas
Khoi, 26, 28
Khoisan-derived peoples, 14, 22, 24
Kirris East, 154
Klein Barmen, 100, 108
Klein Okahandja, 127
Kölnische Zeitung editorial, 60
Kolonialabteilung (Foreign Office), 54
Kolonialblatt, 54, 74
Kolonialrat, 54
Komas Hills, 114

Compositor:	U.C. Press
Printer:	McNaughton & Gunn
Text:	Compset 500 Baskerville
Display:	Compset 500 Andover
Cloth:	Joanna Oxford 64450
Paper:	50 lb. P&S Vellum